Match of My Life

BRIGHTON

KNOW THE SCORE BOOKS SPORTS PUBLICATIONS

CULT HEROES	Author	ISBN
ABERDEEN	Paul Smith	978-1-84818-104-5
CARLISLE UNITED	Mark Harrison	978-1-905449-09-7
CELTIC	David Potter	978-1-905449-08-8
CHELSEA	Leo Moynihan	1-905449-00-3
MANCHESTER CITY	David Clayton	978-1-905449-05-7
NEWCASTLE	Dylan Younger	1-905449-03-8
NOTTINGHAM FOREST	David McVay	978-1-905449-06-4
RANGERS	Paul Smith	978-1-905449-07-1
SOUTHAMPTON	Jeremy Wilson	1-905449-01-1
WEST BROM	Simon Wright	1-905449-02-X

MATCH OF MY LIFE	Editor	ISBN
BRIGHTON	Paul Camillin	978-1-84818-000-0
DERBY COUNTY	Nick Johnson	978-1-905449-68-2
ENGLAND WORLD CUP	Massarella & Moynihan	1-905449-52-6
EUROPEAN CUP FINALS	Ben Lyttleton	1-905449-57-7
FA CUP FINALS 1953-1969	David Saffer	978-1-905449-53-8
FULHAM	Michael Heatley	1-905449-51-8
IPSWICH TOWN	Mel Henderson	978-1-84818-001-7
LEEDS	David Saffer	1-905449-54-2
LIVERPOOL	Leo Moynihan	1-905449-50-X
MANCHESTER UNITED	Ivan Ponting	978-1-905449-59-0
SHEFFIELD UNITED	Nick Johnson	1-905449-62-3
STOKE CITY	Simon Lowe	978-1-905449-55-2
SUNDERLAND	Rob Mason	1-905449-60-7
SPURS	Allen & Massarella	978-1-905449-58-3
WOLVES	Simon Lowe	1-905449-56-9

GENERAL FOOTBALL	Author	ISBN
2006 WORLD CUP DIARY	Harry Harris	1-905449-90-9
ANFIELD OF DREAMS	Neil Dunkin	978-1-905449-80-4
BEHIND THE BACK PAGE	Christopher Davies	978-1-84818-506-7
BOOK OF FOOTBALL OBITUARIES	Ivan Ponting	978-1-905449-82-2
BURKSEY	Peter Morfoot	1-905449-49-6
THE DOOG	Harrison & Gordos	978-1-84818-502-9
FORGIVE US OUR PRESS PASSES	Football Writers' Association	978-1-84818-507-4

HOLD THE BACK PAGE	Harry Harris	1-905449-91-7
JUST ONE OF SEVEN	Denis Smith	978-1-84818-504-3
LEFT BACK IN TIME	Len Ashurst	978-1-84818-512-8
MAN & BABE	Wilf McGuinness	978-1-84818-503-6
MANCHESTER UNITED: PLAYER BY PLAYER		
	Ivan Ponting	978-1-84818-300-1
MY PREMIERSHIP DIARY	Marcus Hahnemann	978-1-905449-33-0
NO SMOKE, NO FIRE	Dave Jones	978-1-84818-513-5
OUTCASTS	Steve Menary	978-1-905449-31-6
The Lands That FIFA Forgot		
PALLY: My Story	Gary Pallister	978-1-84818-500-5
PARISH TO PLANET	Eric Midwinter	978-1-905449-30-9
A History of Football		
PLEASE MAY I HAVE MY FOOTBALL BACK?		
	Eric Alexander	978-1-84818-508-1
THE RIVALS GAME	Douglas Beattie	978-1-905449-79-8
TACKLES LIKE A FERRET	Paul Parker	1-905449-47-X
(England Cover)		
TACKLES LIKE A FERRET	Paul Parker	1-905449-46-1
(Manchester United Cover)		
TOTTENHAM HOTSPUR: PLAYER BY PLAYER		
	Ivan Ponting	978-1-84818-301-8
WARK ON	John Wark	978-1-84818-511-1

RUGBY LEAGUE	Author	ISBN
MOML LEEDS RHINOS	Caplan & Saffer	978-1-905449-69-9
MOML WIGAN WARRIORS	David Kuzio	978-1-905449-66-8

CRICKET	Author	ISBN
ASHES TO DUST	Graham Cookson	978-1-905449-19-4
BEST OF ENEMIES	Kidd & McGuinness	978-1-84818-703-0
BODYLINE HYPOCRISY	Michael Arnold	978-1-84818-702-3
CRASH! BANG! WALLOP!	Martyn Hindley	978-1-905449-88-0
GROVEL!	David Tossell	978-1-905449-43-9
KP: CRICKET GENIUS?	Wayne Veysey	978-1-84818-701-6
MOML: THE ASHES	Pilger & Wightman	1-905449-63-1
MY TURN TO SPIN	Shaun Udal	978-1-905449-42-2
WASTED?	Paul Smith	978-1-905449-45-3

Photographs in this book are reproduced by kind permission of:
Brighton and Hove Albion FC

Front cover:
Top: Jimmy Melia's Brighton team walk out at Wembley to take on Manchester United in the 1983 FA Cup final.
Middle: Manager Russell Slade is carried off the field by exuberant fans after engineering League One survival in 2009.
Bottom: Bobby Zamora and Charlie Oatway celebrate another of Bobby's goals, on the way to the Second Division title.
Rear cover:
Top left: Popular central defender Steve Foster sports his
trademark headband.
Top right: Brighton and Hove Albion FC team group. August 1968 Left to right, back row: Cyril Hodges (trainer), Brian Powney, Nobby Lawton, Norman Gall, John Templeman, John Napier, Charlie Livesey, Jimmy Magill, Tony Burns, Archie Macaulay (manager). Front row: Bobby Smith, Ken Blackburn, Stewart Henderson, Brian Tawse, Paul Flood, Howard Wilkinson, Mike Everitt, Dave Turner.
Bottom: Bobby Zamora fired in the goals which brought two successives championship titles in 2001 and 2002.

Know The Score Books Limited
118 Alcester Road
Studley
Warwickshire
B80 7NT
01527 454482
info@knowthescorebooks.com
www.knowthescorebooks.com

A CIP catalogue record is available for this book from the British Library
ISBN: 978-1-84818-000-0

Jacket design by Graham Hales

Printed and bound in Great Britain
By TJ International

Match of My Life

BRIGHTON

Editor: Paul Camillin

www.knowthescorebooks.com

First published in the United Kingdom
by Know The Score Books Limited, 2009
Copyright Paul Camillin, 2009

Contents

Acknowledgements

Firstly I would like to thank the 15 former Albion players and managers, who each took the time and trouble to provide a chapter for this book. Also, Albion's Life President Dick Knight for kindly writing the foreword. Huge thanks to Simon Levenson for his assistance with editing several of the chapters, and to Bennett Dean, Paul Hazlewood, John Elms, Tim Dudding, and Bill and Jan Swallow for their help in sourcing pictures. Thanks to Tim Carder for his help in checking various facts, figures and trivia from Albion's history - Tim your knowledge is unrivalled; and to Simon Lowe and all those at Know The Score Books for their hard work on getting the book to production.

Editor's Acknowledgements

First and foremost, thanks must go to the players who generously gave their time to contribute a chapter to this book. Their cooperation is much appreciated, as were their efforts on behalf of Brighton & Hove Albion. Between them they achieved an awful lot for our great club – and it is a credit to them that they gave their time to share their thoughts and memories of their time with the club.

Many people have helped enormously with the book, most notably Simon Levenson, who conducted the interviews with Ken Beamish, Danny Cullip, Barry Lloyd and Robbie Reinelt. Big thanks to Tim Carder too, who provided the team line ups and statistical information which compliments each chapter. Tim – along with fellow unsung Albion heroes Bill and Jan Swallow – also assisted with sourcing many of the photos within these pages, and those which adorn the cover.

Also, many thanks to Dick Knight for providing the foreword to the book. Finally thanks to Simon Lowe, Tony Lyons and all those at Know The Score Books for their assistance along the way.

Paul Camillin
August 2009

Introduction

Over the years Brighton & Hove Albion have had many great players and managers, who in their own right have contributed so much to the Brighton & Hove Albion cause. Being asked to select 14 of them, who in turn would select their own special standout match of their Albion careers was not easy.

I feel, with the players' willingness, that the book combines the key Albion personalities with the key games from the club's history. All the post-war promotions are covered, some in great detail – especially 1979, with both Brian Horton and Peter Ward selecting the 3-1 win at Newcastle United, which clinched promotion to the First Division for the first and only time in the club's history.

Adrian Thorne looks back at the club's first-ever League Championship win in 1958; Norman Gall reflects on the club's second title win in 1965; while subsequent promotions in 1972, 1978, 1979 and 1988 are all covered. From the modern era, Danny Cullip and Bobby Zamora look back at the successive championship triumphs in 2001 and 2002, while Charlie Oatway selects the 2004 Play-off Final at the Millenniuim Stadium as his standout game.

Finally, I hope Albion fans will enjoy the read, as much as I have enjoyed editing the book.

Paul Camillin
August 2009

Foreword

There are great moments and great games for every club in every season, but it is those truly exceptional games - to win promotion, avoid relegation, get to Wembley, or games that are not in themselves significant but rock the senses with pure drama, ludicrous goal-gluts, or sensational team or individual performances - that keep us football fans coming back year in, year out.

Albion supporters have had their share of great matches sprinkled through the club's history and most of them are included in this book, which has been written by some of the Seagulls' most famous names.

As you would expect, the late 1970s and early 1980s feature heavily, with Brian Horton, Peter Ward, Gary Williams, Gary Stevens and Steve Foster contributing, but also the vicarious fortunes of the Withdean years you'll find here, with latter day successors Danny Cullip, Bobby Zamora, Charlie Oatway, Guy Butters and Russell Slade each selecting their most memorable Albion match.

I began my love affair with the Albion in the 1940s, and have HD-sharp recall of Adrian Thorne's five-goal salvo - including an eight-minute hattrick! - against Watford one early evening in April 1958 on my 20th birthday. Thorne's opening chapter brings back fond memories for those of us old and lucky enough to have been at the Goldstone that night. In those pre-floodlight days, the game kicked off at 6.15pm, and by about half-past six it was clear that Albion were on their way to their first-ever promotion, 38 years after election to the Football League. Not that my personal 12-year wait for Albion glory was without its moments, but they were mainly crumbs on a bare league table.

By those standards, we've been spoilt ever since, as another championship followed seven years later in 1965 and then promotion in 1972 before the halcyon days began with promotion to the First Division in 1979.

After Wembley in 1983, there was another promotion in 1988 and the club came within 90 minutes of a top-flight return in 1991. After the scandalous sale of the Goldstone Ground in 1995, and subsequent departure two years on, Robbie Reinelt's heroics at Hereford meant that at least the club I had battled for, to lead into exile at Gillingham in 1997, was still clinging to its 77-year membership of the Football League.

After months of hard graft from all of us, we brought the club back to Brighton and in our second year at Withdean, in 2001, we celebrated our third championship title. Who'd have thought the next would only be 12 months away! Our last-seconds play-off win against Swindon, final-day heroics against Ipswich in 2005, and Stockport in 2009, are other memorable Withdean matches included here.

That Stockport match was my final game as Albion chairman, and it was good to end twelve years as chairman on a high note. With Tony Bloom now at the helm, the club is in great shape, the new stadium is on its way ... the culmination of the biggest and hardest game this club and its supporters have ever been involved in.

I have been asked to make my choice for this book. I have been lucky enough to witness many Albion games, including all of those featured here. But I have to say the Albion match of my life has yet to be played. Never will a game have been so long awaited, so fought for the right to be staged, so dreamed about, even played in our minds already ... after all this club has been through in recent years it will come as no surprise to anyone to learn that the first game in our brilliant new stadium will be the Albion Match of My Life.

Dick Knight
Life President

ADRIAN THORNE
FORWARD 1954–1961

BORN 2 August 1937
DEBUT 18 May 1958
ALBION CAREER 84 games, 44 goals

Hove-born Adrian Thorne's name will always stand out in the Brighton history books and for good reason: in just his seventh appearance for the club he hit five goals in what was then the biggest game in the club's history: a thumping 6-0 win over Watford in the Third Division South. It was a vital win which clinched the Albion's first-ever promotion to the old Second Division. An unforgettable night at the Goldstone Ground, it's the one game which stands out from the rest.

Brighton & Hove Albion 6 v Watford 0

League Division Three (South)
Saturday 30 April 1958

Goldstone Ground
Attendance 31,038

Five-goal Thorne clinches promotion for the Seagulls

Teams

Billy Lane	Managers	Neil McBain
Eric Gill	1	Mike Collins
Des Tennant	2	Bobby Bell
Sam Ellis	3	Jack Harrop
Don Bates	4	George Catleugh
Ken Whitfield	5	Vince McNeice
Glen Wilson	6	John Meadows
Dennis Gordon	7	Peter Walker
Adrian Thorne	8	Dave Pygall
Peter Harburn	9	Tommy Anderson
Denis Foreman	10	Sammy Chung
Frankie Howard	11	Willie Devine

Thorne 6, 9, 10, 38, 89, Wilson (pen) 37	Goals	

Referee: J Barradell (Leicestershire)

DESPITE STILL SERVING MY period of National Service in Essex with the army – as was the norm for any young man in the late 1950s – I made my debut for Albion in the January of the 1957/58 promotion season, prior to my being demobbed. The club were very much in the thick of that season's Third Division South title race – as they had been for much of the 1950s. I remember my first match, away at Southend United, being a good one and it stands out not just because it was my debut, but also because we won the game at Roots Hall quite comfortably by two goals to nil to maintain the club's promotion push. We were two points ahead of Swindon in the scrap for the only promotion spot available from the Division at that time, with two games in hand, so it was a vital victory. Popular winger Frankie Howard got one goal and I was delighted to score on my debut to seal what was a fairly routine win and make a nice start to life with the first team.

Being a serving soldier, before the match I had to get permission from the army to play in the game – but that was fairly straightforward in those days. During National Service, players who were registered professionals with Football League clubs had an unwritten deal with the army that allowed them to play for their clubs at weekends. The Colonel in charge of the Command football team had agreed that with all the various officers as long as the players were prepared to play midweek in the inter-unit games. Everything would then be organised so that you didn't have to undertake any weekend army duties and you would be given a 48-hour pass from Friday night through to Sunday evening to be able to go and play football for your club.

I was billeted at Colchester barracks and thanks to that unwritten agreement I was able to get weekends off, travel back to Hove and play for Albion's reserve side – and then on a few occasions the first-team – while I was completing my service with the army. At that point I had been scoring a few goals in the Combination League for the reserves and it was a result of my form in the reserves that the club's manager Billy Lane called me up to play for the first team at Southend. I remember Roots Hall had quite a large pitch and we used that to our advantage. The team I came into were playing very well anyway. They'd only lost one of the previous seven games, which included two 5-2 home wins, over Colchester United and Gillingham.

What I recall of the actual match was that I really enjoyed it. I found that I got a lot of the ball and that it was pretty easy to slot into the team in that one particular game. From what I can remember everything went well, certainly the result suggests that.

Having come into the first team for that match, I played two more. My second match was a goalless draw against Norwich City at Carrow Road, and the third was my home debut. That was a 1-1 draw with Southampton at the Goldstone Ground, a game in which I got my second Albion goal as we fought back from being a goal down at half-time to pick up an important point against Saints, who were one of our main promotion rivals at that point in the season, as well as being south coast rivals. After three successive games I was then rested. I was only a youngster after all.

Six days after the Southampton match, I completed my National Service and I was demobilised from the army on 14th February 1958 – an easy date to remember, being Valentine's Day. I resumed full-time training at the club, but it wasn't until April that I ended up having another run in the team. Towards the end of the campaign inside-forward Dave Sexton, who was having a great season, was ruled out with an injury he had picked up in a match at Port Vale, and I came in and took his place.

The club had been very close to promotion the two previous seasons and you could say they were experienced at failure to win promotion to the Second Division, finishing sixth in 1956/57 and a close second in the previous campaign, just one point behind champions Leyton Orient, and with a better goal difference. Having said that, everyone felt that 1957/58 was finally going to be the season when the club stepped up to that level. I can't explain it, but there was a confidence running through the players, staff and even the supporters. Everyone had experienced doing very well in previous seasons, but falling just short at the last moments. Suddenly we all felt this was going to be it, this was to be our time and we were eventually proved to be quite right.

Having been back in the reserves, apart from one match when I'd been with the first-team squad in mid-April at Torquay, I returned to the side at the end of April with three games left to play – two against Watford sandwiching a game at Brentford – and the club's promotion fate very much in the players' hands. First we beat Watford 1-0 at Vicarage Road on Saturday 26th April, thanks to a last-minute goal from Denis Foreman. It was a vital victory as it meant a point from the next two games would clinch the championship and promotion to the Second Division as no-one else could achieve more than the 58 points we had already earned.

After the match our manager Billy Lane – who had actually missed the winning goal as he was making his way down to the dressing room from the stands and was greeted on his arrival with the news we'd won thanks to Denis's strike – told us he would be sticking with the same team for the next two matches. He didn't want to make any changes, because it was such a delicate situation and he was confident we would do the job required. I think his thinking was 'they've got this far, let them see if they can do it. They can live or die by the results!'

We then played Brentford, needing just that one point to clinch the huge prize on offer with one game to spare, at Griffin Park on the Monday evening. It was a massive game as Brentford were only two points behind us, but had just this one game remaining. If they won, as they had a better goal average than us, they would top the table. Unfortunately we went a goal down during the second half. Towards the end of the game, with very little time left to play, centre-forward Peter Harburn played a perfect pass through to me and I went past the full-back, who'd come to tackle me, the goalkeeper came out and I pushed the ball past the keeper for a great goal. . . but the referee gave me as offside. It was a shocking decision, especially as a draw would have been enough to have clinched the championship. The 1-0 defeat left us sitting in third position behind Brentford and Swindon, who both now had better goal averages than us, and we still needed that vital final point from an ever more vital final game.

That night at Griffin Park was the greatest level of disappointment I have ever felt in my life. It was quite unbelievable, but the decision stood and we had to face Watford on the Wednesday evening knowing we had one more chance to clinch glory. Thankfully – playing in front of our home fans – that turned out to be a positive result for us and an unforgettable night at the Goldstone Ground.

We'd had to cram our last five games into the last 11 days of the season, because in those days the season had to be finished by the end of April – but you didn't have the situation you have nowadays where everybody plays their final fixture at the same time on the same day. Our game was literally the only outstanding match to be played – everybody else had finished their fixtures. It was perfectly set up and in some ways the short period between the disappointment of Brentford and having this last opportunity to put things right helped as we didn't have any time to dwell on things.

We trained on the Tuesday, which was a very light session, and there were no injuries in the Brentford match so we kept the same team for the Wednesday. Floodlights were yet to be installed at the Goldstone in 1958, and, being a light April evening, the match kicked off at 6.15pm. There was a capacity crowd of over 30,000 inside the Goldstone and a real sense of anticipation amongst the crowd – although after enduring several disappointments in recent years they were not counting any chickens ahead of the kick-off.

I can remember running out of the tunnel onto the field with Billy Lane's words ringing in my head. He simply said, "Off you go, you know what to do" – and as we ran out, led by our captain Glen Wilson, I could sense the determination in the team. Glen was a superb skipper: a hard, efficient, tireless worker in midfield. He, with Don Bates and Kenny Whitfield, formed a superb midfield trio throughout that season and stopped any sort of attacks from Watford that night.

Up front we tore them apart, annihilating them with three quick goals inside the first ten minutes. Bang, bang, bang. Effectively the game was over. It was sheer determination that gave us such a stunning start to the match and from memory Watford didn't provide any threat at any stage in the game. It was almost as if they had mentally withdrawn and lost the combat factor that is necessary to compete in, let alone win or draw, a football match. Let's face it, 3-0 down away from home to a club on the brink of promotion, with a massive crowd urging on the home side, that's a very difficult hurdle to overcome.

On a personal note it was an unforgettable evening for me, but I wouldn't say it was my best performance for the club: on the night the ball seemed to break favourably for me and the openings just appeared and I ended up scoring five goals in a six-nil win which clinched promotion.

But I still maintain that I have played lots of better games than that and never scored. Other times I've bagged plenty of goals. I once scored four against Bristol Rovers at the Goldstone in 1960, and that was a much harder game and it was more difficult to score the four against Bristol than it was to get the five against Watford. It's strange as a goalscorer. If things break for you – like a batsman or a bowler, if they're on form they get runs or take wickets – sometimes everything goes for you. Perhaps it was fate – that the club were destined for promotion having missed out in previous seasons – and simply everything slotted nicely into place. We could have played the same match, with the same players, a week later and it would probably have been a completely different game, a goalless draw. As it was it was a triumph for the club, the supporters, and, thankfully, me.

I remember for the first goal. Peter Harburn was involved. The ball was played up to him and he tried to chest in down, but it came off his chest and broke to me about 12 yards out and all I did was run on to the ball and just hit it into the goal. The perfect start, early on. And all through a bit of a lucky break.

The second was a cross from Frankie Howard. He got the ball on the wing and the defence just left me unmarked as they moved to defend the goal. I had a clear header at goal from Frankie's perfect cross and I remember watching that goal very clearly: in it went to the top corner.

I don't remember much about the third goal – except it was close in and the ball broke kindly for me again. Glen Wilson then scored a penalty and I added another to the tally before half-time. Watford played like defeated players; they had lost their momentum and the second half was very comfortable, like an evening stroll in the park and the players and the crowd were able to enjoy the occasion.

My fifth and final goal came late in the game and at the final whistle I can remember quite clearly that I couldn't get off the pitch and into the dressing room. The supporters had come onto the pitch from all sides and it was like Rorke's Drift – we were surrounded not by Zulus, but Brighton fans. Blue and white scarves and delighted faces were all around, swamping us. I remember the police having to clear a path to get us all off.

We had won promotion and although I only played a handful of games I felt I had played an important part in that. Everyone was obviously delighted with the result and what it meant, after years of trying for Second Division football: the directors, the players, the supporters and the town in general. All the directors and other notables came down to the dressing room to toast promotion with champagne and I think after that all the players were individually called up into the West Stand and presented to the crowd. I know I was dragged up there.

Brighton, as it is today, was always popular with entertainers, actors and actresses, and the town's local celebrities were all in attendance that night. I can remember Max Miller, the music hall comedian, Fred Emery and Anna Needles were all amongst the invited guests in the stand. I was still rather muddy and dishevelled when I was called up to the stand to be presented and I remember, I didn't kiss her, she kissed me but I apologised straight away to her for being in such a filthy state!

After the presentation and, what in those days was a very rare filmed, post-match interview alongside Billy Lane – possibly for showing on the old cinema newsreels or maybe on television – I went out to celebrate with a couple of drinks in the pub on the corner of Sackville Road. Today it's the Sackville or the Hove Park Tavern, but it was known back then as the Old Shoreham Pub. A lot of the players were there – Denis Foreman, Frankie Howard, Dennis Gordon, Kenny Whitfield – plus a lot of the players who hadn't played on the night, but had contributed over the season like Dave Sexton, who, of course, had missed the match with injury, and some of the older players like Bobby Farrell. The landlord was an Albion supporter, so it was virtually drinks on the house all night and there was a lot of excitement as we all gradually lost touch with reality. For a few hours we couldn't get out of the pub because it was surrounded by supporters celebrating the promotion! Eventually proceedings were brought to a close by a friend of Denis Foreman – a priest who had come to England from South Africa – who had come to Brighton to watch Denis play. I remember him more or less advising Denis and myself that we'd had enough to drink! I didn't feel too well and I know Denis didn't, and it is safe to say a lot of the Albion players came out of that pub quite inebriated.

There were a few club officials there too, but the boss Billy Lane – a teetotaller – was absent. He left the Goldstone Ground shortly after the match with a bunch of red roses and the legend is he went to Hove Cemetery to place the flowers on the grave of Major Carlo Campbell – the former Albion chairman. The Major was buried there, and Billy Lane had had a very good working relationship with him. Major Carlo had supported Billy when things hadn't been going too well in previous seasons and Billy felt he should go and thank Major Campbell for his help in achieving the success we had enjoyed that evening. He put much of that down to the support of this man over the years.

About a fortnight later Brighton Town Council gave us a reception in the Royal Pavilion. It is a superb place with the Indian theme which was all the rage in the early 19th century. It was a great night and we had a superb meal there. Then, not long after that, we had another reception at Hove Town Hall, which has burned down now, with Hove Town Council. It was a slightly different format, with all different people coming up and speaking about the game and others singing songs, and then at the end all the players were presented with a wrist watch, cuff links and a tie – and I was given an silver cup, engraved with the match and date. After that it was similar situation to the one at the Old Shoreham pub.

After helping the club win promotion to the Second Division I spent a further three seasons with Albion and, despite an inauspicious start to life at that level the following August – we lost 9-0 at Middlesbrough in a match in which the late Brian Clough scored five times – we fared pretty well for new boys in the Second Division. After such a terribly start – we only won one of our first ten matches – we recovered to finish in a very respectable 12th in the table. It was one place higher than Middlesbrough, who took their tally of goals against us to 15 for the season when they put six past us at the Goldstone in a 6-4 win, although Cloughie only got a hat-trick that day!

In our second season in the Second Division we finished 14th and followed that with a 16th-placed finish in 1960/61. Both Billy Lane and I left the club in the summer of 1961, having top scored that season with 14 goals – and I ended my Albion career with a record of 44 goals in 84 Albion games, better than a goal every other game, having played as a forward, winger, outside-left and outside-right. After leaving the Goldstone, I moved west to Devon and joined Plymouth Argyle for £8000. There were more adventures to be had in Devon with Exeter City, before further moves to Leyton Orient, and Cheltenham Town and Barnet – both non-league clubs in those days – before I hung up the old boots and moved into teaching. But having scored five goals on that glorious night when we hit Watford for six of the best – in one of the biggest game in the club's history – will always stand out as the match of my life.

NORMAN GALL
CENTRE-HALF 1962–1974

BORN   30 September 1942
DEBUT   29 September 1962
ALBION CAREER   488 games, 4 goals

To older fans, centre-half Norman Gall needs little introduction. A one-club player, he racked up 488 appearances for Brighton over a 12-year period between 1962 and 1974, helping the Seagulls to promotion to the Third Division in 1965 and the Second Division in 1972. Younger fans will be more familiar with him – or at least his voice – as the expert summariser on Albion's match commentaries on BBC radio.

Rochdale 2 v Brighton & Hove Albion 2

League Division Four
Monday 22 March 1965

Spotland
Attendance 7,005

A red card for Gall, but a vital point for the Albion as they march towards the Fourth Division title

Teams

Tony Collins	Managers	Archie Macauley
Ted Burgin	1	Brian Powney
Roy Ridge	2	Mel Hopkins
Laurie Calloway	3	Bobby Baxter
Arthur Cunliffe	4	Barrie Rees
Ray Aspden	5	Norman Gall
Jmmy Thompson	6	Dave Turner
Brian Birch	7	Wally Gould
George Morton	8	Jimmy Collins
Bert Lister	9	Jack Smith
Reg Jenkins	10	Jim Oliver
Don McKenzie	11	Johnny Goodchild
Thompson pen 21, Morton 46	Goals	Goodchild 3, Collins 51
Lister 75	Sent Off	Gall 75

Referee: K Howley

BEING ASKED TO SELECT the match of my life from my time with the Albion isn't easy and was something I had to give a fair amount of thought. I was lucky enough to play in a few high-profile matches for the club: promotion-clinching games against Darlington and Rochdale, a famous FA Cup tie against Chelsea at the Goldstone in 1967. There were also the club's record-breaking league and cup wins, both within the space of 14 days; a 9-1 thumping of Southend in Division Three and a 10-1 hammering of Wisbech Town in the FA Cup. Despite not managing to score even one of the nineteen goals Albion scored in those games, I was selected as the *Evening Argus* man-of-the-match on both occasions – how that happened to this day I still don't know, with all the goals flying in at the other end, but I suppose I must have been doing something right out there!

However the match I settled on stands out in my mind for different reasons to those you might expect: it was a bruising encounter against Rochdale at Spotland in 1964/65, the year we won the old fourth division championship. Firstly, it was a game against one of our promotion rivals, a match in which we were pleased to get a vital point in our quest for the championship, but, possibly you might think strangely, it was also one in which I was shown the red card; and one which subsequently landed me in the dock before a Lancashire judge and saw my name splashed across all the national papers!

I joined the Albion in 1962 from Gateshead. The move came off the back of two FA Cup ties in which Gateshead, then a non-league team, had performed well against Football League opponents. I had acquitted myself well and the papers began to link me with moves to various league clubs. As a youngster I had played for the now-famed Wallsend Boys Football Club – which over the years has produced several top players, including Alan Shearer, Lee Clark, Steve Bruce, Michael Carrick and Peter Beardsley. In those days we were linked to Gateshead and the team represented them in the FA Youth Cup. One game that stands out from junior football with Wallsend is a win over my favourite team Newcastle United.

The natural progression was to step up into the first team at Gateshead and my opportunity came with an injury to Graham Carr – he went onto have a very good career in league football playing for Northampton Town and later managing them; he is also the father of the famous comedian Alan Carr, of *The Friday Night Project* on Channel 4. I was only expected to fill in for Graham, but once I got into the team I wanted to stay there and thankfully I had a few good performances at centre-half and managed to do just that. By November 1961, at the age of 19, I had established myself as a regular in the side.

With this being non-league football I had to have a job to pay the rent. I was working as an apprentice draughtsman and was on course to qualify as a marine engineer, but having had such success with Gateshead I began to think to myself that football could also provide me with a very good career and I had strong ambitions to break into league football. I was an amateur with Gateshead – who although a non-league club playing in the Northern Premier League, had only recently been demoted from the Football League. They had actually offered me the opportunity of signing professional forms, but I had my heart set on signing for a Football League club and those FA Cup games provided me with the perfect opportunity to put myself in the shop window.

In round one we were drawn away to Tranmere Rovers who were mid-table in the old Fourth Division, but on a good run of form – but we beat them 3-2 in a terrific match on the Wirral. Whenever I have been back to Prenton Park with the Albion – either as a player or commentator – it always evokes strong memories for me of that great day with Gateshead.

That was easily the biggest match of my life at that time. There was a big crowd in the ground and the home side put us under a lot of pressure to start with, but we settled down and scored two goals before half-time and we were cruising. We scored again in the second half to go three up, but Tranmere came back strongly at us late in the game and pulled the score back to 3-2. We were under real pressure for the last ten minutes, but myself and my defensive partner Jackie Heron held firm. That did me the world of good as I got a lot of good reports and it sparked a bit of interest.

In round two we were drawn at home to Workington – who were also in the Fourth Division. The Lancashire side ended our dream of a third-round tie against one of the glamour clubs – the likes of Wolves, Burnley, Spurs or Liverpool in those days – but for me personally I had enjoyed the two games and was fortunate enough to have been named man-of-the-match in both ties which led to great press speculation about my future. It was exciting reading my name in the paper alongside the names of some of the country's top clubs – I still have the cuttings today. Blackpool – then in the top-flight of English football – was the standout name, but there were other big clubs: Preston North End, Southampton and Middlesbrough. There were other lower-league clubs: Carlisle, Northampton Town and Bury said to be interested, but it was Brighton & Hove Albion who stood out for me. They were then in the old Second Division and it was arranged that my father and I would drive down to meet with the then-manager George Curtis. I got a good feeling about Brighton. I had been to see both Preston and Blackpool and they seemed very similar to Newcastle – but having seen Brighton on television I was drawn by the fact it was so different to what I was used to. I fancied the change and the chance of experiencing something new. We drove down, met Mr Curtis and I signed there and then in March 1962.

I liked George, but it's fair to say he had a pretty disastrous time at the Albion. I remember sitting in the West Stand for the first game after I signed and Newcastle hammered Albion out of sight by four goals to nil. The following week the team lost at Middlesbrough by the same score and a few weeks later Albion were relegated to the Third Division. The following season – in which I was playing regularly for the reserves and played five games for the first team – we were relegated again to the bottom division, so it was it was tough for George, but I will always be grateful for him for bringing me to the club and giving me my chance.

In April 1963, with relegation all but mathematically confirmed, George Curtis was sacked and the club appointed Archie Macaulay as manager. It was under Archie that I broke into the first team and began to play regularly the following season. Before establishing myself in the side, I was playing mostly for the reserves and had moved into digs not far from the ground. I lived in Goldstone Lane and my room overlooked the ground.

During Archie's first full season in charge, 1963/64, I played 41 games. We had a decent season, finishing eighth, and but for an awful run of form through the winter months of December and January could have been in the promotion shake up. However we had laid good foundations for the following season and along with the supporters we were confident we could win promotion in 1964/65.

The arrival of Bobby Smith from Spurs that summer made national headlines and further raised both those expectations and the confidence within the players already at the club. Bobby had won the league and FA

Cup double with Spurs in 1961 and was an England international (Smith scored 13 goals for England and had won the last of 15 caps for his country the previous November in an 8-3 win over Northern Ireland) and it was a major coup for a Fourth Division side to sign an England player! The arrival of Bobby really put the club on the map and the team in the spotlight and having such a quality player in the same team worked wonders for all of us.

We made an indifferent start to the season and even dropped as low as 13th during October, but a terrific second half of the season saw us lose just four times between the end of November and the end of the season. By the time we arrived at Spotland in late March to take on Rochdale, one of our promotion rivals, we were in the fourth and final promotion place and looking a good bet for promotion. Dale were just a point behind us in fifth and looking the most likely club to push us.

I think some games you will remember forever. Good games, good goals. This was a cracking game, but I can't remember much detail from it, apart from it being quite a tetchy affair – which wasn't helped by some poor refereeing. I remember their first goal, early on, was extremely controversial as referee Kevin Howley initially awarded a goal, but then seemed to back track. The reason for that was that we were incensed as we knew the ball had not crossed the line – our keeper Brian Powney had punched it away – and the linesman backed us up by telling Mr Howley it wasn't a goal. So instead he awarded Rochdale a penalty, claiming an Albion defender had punched the ball out from under the crossbar, when in fact it had been Brian. We were livid, and all the more so when the penalty was converted.

We fought back to equalise through Johnny Goodchild – only for Rochdale to retake the lead. Jimmy Collins equalised for us a second time, before the incident occurred which makes the game stand out in my mind as certainly the most eventful of my career.

Myself and the Rochdale forward Bert Lister – a big stocky six-foot-plus centre-forward – were chasing a loose ball towards the by-line in front of the main stand at Spotland. As we were running towards the ball I knew what he was going to do; I knew he wasn't going to go for the ball – so neither did I. I stood my ground and we both barged each other. He went into the wall and I went over the top and into the home supporters. As I went into the crowd I felt a blow to the back of my head. As I got to my feet, still in the crowd, and found everyone was trying to hit me. I had my head down and couldn't see much and I put my hands up to protect myself, instinctively pushing out at the baying mob. I managed to get away from the crowd and back onto the side of the pitch, but then Lister started wrestling with me. We were both on the ground for a few seconds before the other players ran in to separate us and stop us fighting. Howley came over and straight away sent us both off. Lister went off being cheered by the Rochdale fans, and I was told by Jimmy Collins the captain to go down injured so they could buy some time and reorganise the defence. That upset the crowd even more. Thomas then ordered me to get off and by then I was getting some real stick from the crowd.

Archie Macaulay came out to put his arm around me and console me, but as we were walking off the pitch towards the tunnel we were pelted with rubbish, fruit, pies and all sorts by their fans. At that point Archie bailed out and left me to walk back to the dressing room on my own, taking sanctuary in the dug-out. I took the brunt of the supporters' pelting as I left the field of play and I remember sitting down in the dressing room and looking down at my shirt. It was covered in rubbish – but at the same time I was thinking how important the point could be.

When the lads came back in and we'd hung on for a 2-2 draw, I remember just being really pleased. Fortunately the manager wasn't angry with me. I knew I would have to serve a suspension for the sending off, but I wasn't too bothered; at that point in the season I was more happy with a valuable point against one of our main promotion rivals.

I didn't give the sending off much more thought after the game and the following day I was enjoying a pint in the local when the barman called me up to the bar and told me there was a phone call for me. On the other end of the line was a reporter from *The People* who asked me how I felt about being charged with assaulting a spectator the previous day. I don't know how he tracked me down to the pub, but he explained the police were charging me for assaulting one of the Rochdale supporters a Mr Southlands. I was amazed.

I was summoned to court, and travelled back up to Greater Manchester with Harold Paris, one of the club's directors. Archie Macaulay met up with us when we got there. I wasn't too worried – I knew I hadn't done anything wrong – but I was still nervous. I was asked to explain what had happened, so I told the story of how the game had been a very lively one and that I had fallen into the crowd after the challenge with Lister. I knew I had hit someone with my arm, but it was in self defence and I was more intent with getting away from the supporters and back onto the pitch to continue the game than picking a fight with them.

As I expected, I was found not guilty. It was still a relief when it was all over. I shook hands with Mr Southlands. He told me he hadn't wanted to make a fuss and press charges, but the police had made him do it. He was invited down to the Goldstone by the club for a game – I remember him coming and having a drink with him after the match.

I hadn't told my family anything about the court case. I knew my dad wouldn't be too happy about it, regardless of my innocence, but he found out that evening, via a story in the local paper. It was in the *Newcastle Journal* and I was on the back page – even up there! My father phoned me and asked me what it was all about. As expected, he didn't like it and he wasn't very happy, but I explained it to him and he half accepted my apology.

I served a seven-day suspension and missed two matches, at home to Southport and away at Oxford. On reflection it wasn't really the referee's fault that I got sent off, but he did have a bad game, starting with a dreadful decision for Rochdale's first goal, and he lost control of proceedings in my opinion. After I was sent off I was under a lot of pressure coming off the pitch – but the result was the main thing, the only thing. We knew we had a very good chance of promotion and that point turned out to be an important one come the end of the season.

We went top of the league by beating Tranmere 2-1 at the Goldstone Ground in early April – and I scored the winning goal in the last minute of the game. Tranmere were another one of our main promotion rivals, and had gone 1-0 up after I made a mistake with a short back pass which let in their striker to score – but Bobby Smith drew us level and I then headed in a corner in the final minute at the south-stand end. Wally Gould picked me out from the left and I got above the Rovers defence and headed home.

That win took us above our opponents and put us at the head of the division with four games to play. We won two out of the next three, and went into the final game of the season needing a point against Darlington at the Goldstone to secure top spot. We were confident, and I knew that we were too good for them and we were proved right. We won comfortably 3-1 to clinch promotion as champions.

We had a terrific side that season. We had real experience up front. Leading the line were Bobby Smith and Wally Gould – but we had a young defence in Barrie Rees, Dave Turner and myself, in front of little Brian Powney in goal, who was small for a keeper. But we felt we were good enough and we knew we could win the championship. That was the most important thing for me that season and getting that point at Rochdale contributed to that.

That was one of the best sides the Albion had. People still come up to me now and say that it was their favourite or most exciting season.

In 1972 I won promotion with the club a second time, from the Third to the Second Division. That was a slightly different feeling – and it didn't feel the same as 1965. It might have been because I was older and more experienced, but I didn't get the same buzz as I had from the first promotion. Our main rivals were Aston Villa – who had fallen very quickly from the First Division to the Third – and I remember beating them at the Goldstone in front of the Match of the Day cameras, with Willie Irvine scoring a great goal.

Ironically, at the end of the 1971/72 season, we clinched promotion thanks to another draw with Rochdale. We had to get a point to win promotion and they needed a point to avoid relegation: unsurprisingly it was a 1-1 draw in what was one of the strangest games I ever played in. We led 1-0 at half-time thanks to John Templeman's first-half strike, but Rochdale equalised in the second half and when they did it shook us up a bit. From that point, the two managers in each dugout were calling everybody back into defence to make sure we didn't lose. There were basically two teams camped in their own halves. There was no chance of any more goals being scored and we both got the result we needed.

That was another great game which stands out when I look back at my career – but for some reason the Rochdale game from 1965 is the one which really lingers in my memory.

KEN BEAMISH
CENTRE-FORWARD 1972–1974

BORN   25 August 1947
DEBUT   15 March 1972
ALBION CAREER   99 games, 28 goals

Ken Beamish became Brighton's record signing in March 1972, when Pat Saward brought him from Tranmere to the Goldstone for a £25,000 fee, with Alan Duffy moving in the opposite direction. He soon became a fans' favourite, scoring some spectacular late goals as he helped the Albion win a place in the old Second Division for the first time in a decade. He was the type of striker any club would value, with his never say die attitude and the ability to score goals from anywhere. Ken was with the club for two years, scoring 28 goals from a total of 99 appearances.

Brighton & Hove Albion 1 v Rochdale 1

League Division Three
Wednesday 3 May 1972

Goldstone Ground
Attendance 34,766

A tense draw secures promotion for Beamish and the Albion on a memorable night at the Goldstone Ground

Teams

Pat Saward	Managers	Dick Conner
Brian Powney	1	Tony Godfrey
Bert Murray	2	Ronnie Blair
Eddie Spearritt	3	Bobby Downes
John Templeman	4	Peter Gowans
Ian Goodwin	5	Colin Parry
Norman Gall	6	Arthur Marsh
Kit Napier	7	Tony Buck
(Sub. Bertie Lutton)		
Ken Beamish	8	Reg Jenkins
Willie Irvine	9	Alf Arrowsmith
Brian Bromley	10	Len Kinsella
Peter O'Sullivan	11	Malcolm Darling
Templeman 3	Goals	Gowans 60

Referee: J Taylor (Wolverhampton)

AFTER PLAYING FOR CHESHIRE and Liverpool schools I joined Tranmere Rovers as a part-time player in July 1966, at the age of 18. At the time I was by no means certain that football would be the career for me, so I served my time as an apprentice toolmaker at a local engineering company at the same time. The last 12 months of my apprenticeship were spent in the drawing office, and I was heading down the road to becoming a fully-qualified draughtsman, but Tranmere came in with an offer of a full-time contract, so I put the drawing office on the back burner, knowing I could always return to that trade if the football career didn't work out.

I spent six years at Prenton Park and enjoyed every bit of my time there. By the time I left I had played 176 games for them and scored 49 goals. All the players used to read the columns in the Sunday papers, and I was forever being linked with a move away from Tranmere. One week it would be Liverpool that would be on verge of making an offer for me, the next week I would read that Everton wanted to buy me. It was getting close to transfer deadline day when the move to Brighton came up. Coventry City – then in the old First Division - had just had an offer rejected by the club, but I remember there was a lad named Alan Duffy on the books at the Goldstone, and he was involved in the deal that took me to Brighton. He was out of favour, and Tranmere were very keen on him moving in the opposite direction as a replacement for me.

The deal was touch and go, and very nearly didn't happen. I only met manager Pat Saward to sort out the details of the move on transfer deadline day. We sat and sorted everything out in a Manchester hotel, and the papers were rushed off to the Football League headquarters, then based in nearby Lytham St Annes, with less than an hour to go to the deadline; thankfully they arrived before the 5pm cut-off point.

It was the right move for me at the time as I felt that Brighton, then in the Third Division promotion race, were a club that were going places under Pat Saward. Tranmere had always just bobbed about in the lower leagues, and were too much in the shadow of Liverpool and Everton to really progress in the way that Brighton eventually did.

Pat Saward was a great character and it makes me smile when I see club sponsors asking fans to take part in competitions to help buy players, as if it's something new that they've just thought up. I wonder how many of them realise that it's old hat and that Pat was the instigator of getting fans involved in that sort of thing. Bert Murray, who the club bought from the proceeds of Pat's buy-a-player-fund, was certainly a big influence in the team. I had a lot of time for Pat: he had a big bloke image and he knew his football.

I arrived at the club on the Thursday and found myself on the substitute's bench for my first game against Oldham at the Goldstone. Having only been at the club for two days, I wasn't really expecting to get into the starting line-up straight away. I was impressed with the atmosphere that the fans generated and there was a crowd of nearly 18,000 hoping to see another home victory. It wasn't to be that day, though. The game was a bit flat and it was one of those days when we were never going to score. I remember coming on to replace Willie Irvine in an effort to salvage something, but Oldham ended up winning by the only goal of the game. We lost the next game at Bradford City as well, and once again I had to be content with a substitute's role.

We were still third in the table and everyone at the club was confident that we would win promotion. They weren't going to let a couple of bad defeats ruin what had been an excellent season. There was a very good bunch of lads there. Norman Gall, Eddie Spearritt, John Templeman and Peter O'Sullivan were all good players who had confidence in their own abilities, while big John Napier who played at centre-half, stands out in the memory as another very important player for us. With Aston Villa running away with the league it was always going to be a battle for the second promotion place between our chief rivals, Bournemouth, Notts County and us. The play-offs hadn't been invented then so there were no second chances if you finished outside the top two.

As luck would have it our next game was against Aston Villa at the Goldstone and I finally made my first start. They were, and still are, a massive club who should never have been playing in that division. But they were and we were determined to bounce back from the poor run. Pat Saward decided to make changes and dropped both full-back Stewart Henderson and John Napier from the defence. Ian Goodwin was brought back in after a long injury lay-off and Bert Murray switched to right-back, allowing me to play up front with Kit Napier and Willie Irvine. It was a brave move from Pat but it certainly paid off.

The *Match of the Day* cameras were at the ground and there was an expectant buzz around the Goldstone as the teams took the field. Willie Irvine's goal was an absolute cracker and a brilliant team effort and it fully deserved to take its place as one of the goals of the season. But for all the great build-up, Willie still had to hit the target and he did so brilliantly. Willie is a lovely bloke and I still see him from time to time at Burnley where he does a bit of work.

It was a very important win and it just showed the quality of the team that we could not only compete with teams of the calibre of Aston Villa, but also beat them. We were unbeaten against them that season, as we'd already drawn 0-0 at Villa Park before I joined. My first goal arrived against Torquay at the Goldstone on Good Friday. I do remember we were losing at half-time but I don't remember the goal at all. I know Bertie Lutton, who'd been on loan prior to signing permanently just before I arrived at the club, scored one of the goals. In those days the Easter programme was rather more hectic than it is now and we played three games in the space of four or five days. It was tiring, but it was the same for everyone.

The match the following day was the really important one, as we were away to our biggest rivals, Bournemouth. As a player Dean Court was always a successful ground for me. It didn't matter which club I was playing for, be it Tranmere or Brighton we always seemed to come away with a decent result. It was important that we didn't lose the game, and we were the better side throughout. Despite that, we were losing at half-time, before Bertie Lutton scored a deserved equaliser. We left there thinking it was a point dropped rather than one gained, and still we couldn't break into the top two.

But the result against Aston Villa had given the whole team a big boost of confidence, and my partnership with Willie Irvine was really starting to bear fruit. We had a great away record that season, and scored over forty goals which were not only a great achievement, but also testimony to the way Pat Saward liked his teams to play football.

I felt I was in a run of great form, confident of shooting from anywhere, although it didn't always come off. We went up to Barnsley for the third of our Easter fixtures and John Templeman scored the winner to put us into second place. I hit two goals against Wrexham the following Saturday and also scored in the 3-0 win over Blackburn. As the end of the season drew closer the crowds at the Goldstone were growing larger and larger and there were certainly over 20,000 fans at each of the last four home games.

We quite often left it late to score the winning goals and never more so than against Rotherham in the penultimate home game. It was 1-1 and we were well into injury time when I received the ball about thirty yards out from goal. I am sure their goalkeeper was expecting anything but a shot, so when I let fly he was caught off guard. It was the sort of shot that 99 times out of 100 would have ended up in the crowd, but fortunately I struck it well, the keeper fluffed it and it ended up in the net to give us the win we needed.

There were just two games left, both against Rochdale – and one of those proved to be the Match of My Life for the club. Rochdale were caught up in a relegation battle. Torquay and Bradford were both almost certain to go down, but our opponents were one of about six teams who could also find themselves relegated. Added to that, we knew that a win and a draw from those two games would see us promoted. The first match was at Spotland and again yours truly scored a late goal after it looked like we would have to settle for draw. I'm told it's the last time the Albion have ever won at Rochdale, but to be honest I don't remember a thing about the goal that gave us a 2-1 win.

That set up the final game of the season on Wednesday 3 May 1972. We needed a point for promotion, and coincidentally a point for Rochdale would see them stay in the Third Division for another season.

Pat Saward was always meticulous in his preparation for games. We were taken to a hotel in Brighton for a pre-match meal, and, knowing there would be a large crowd at the Goldstone, left slightly earlier than usual to avoid the traffic. As it turned out we arrived at the ground later than normal, because of the unbelievable amount of fans heading to the match.

It was an amazing experience walking out in front of such a large crowd. We were used to good support at the Goldstone but to be playing for promotion in front of 34,000 people was different to anything I'd experienced. You don't often get Third Division games with a full house and it was an occasion I'll never ever forget.

I remember we went in front though John Templeman early on, but we couldn't find a way through their defence to get a second goal and ease the tension. Their equaliser came right out of the blue in the second half. One of their players just let fly and the ball screamed into the net over Brian Powney's head.

With about 20 minutes to go, the game suddenly died a death. As things stood we had the point we needed to win promotion and they were safe from relegation. With hand on heart I can say it was never in our plans just to play the game out; it just materialised. Neither side had a shot on goal in those final minutes, nor did either team look to penetrate each other's defence. It probably wouldn't happen nowadays because the final matches of the season are all played on the same day, but back then we were playing after the end of the regular season and so both knew what we had to do.

When the final whistle eventually blew virtually the whole crowd came on the to the playing area and we ran off the pitch to the safety of the dressing room as fast as we could. We made our way to the directors' box to acknowledge the fans and threw our shirts into the crowd. Later we made our way into Brighton and went to one of the big hotels on the seafront to celebrate. I think it was called the Kings Hotel. The manager was an Albion fan and he always made sure we were looked after there. I do remember that it was dawn before I eventually made my way home. What a fantastic night!

During that summer we carried on partying and we used to often go to a cabaret club that I think was owned by Mike Bamber. He certainly had a share in the place and we used it for team bonding during the following season. When you look back at it the club were quite forward thinking at the time. As a team we were hopeful of bigger things to come but it never came off for that squad, nor for me personally and it was a pity we came unstuck the following year.

I was top scorer in the 1972/73 season, but I can't put my finger on why we played so badly. We had decent players with George Ley from Portsmouth at left-back. I really don't know why it didn't click for us, as we were certainly a better team than the results showed that season.

After we were relegated back to the Third Division Pat Saward came under increasing pressure in the early months of the 1973/74 season and with our home form pretty awful, it was no real surprise when the board decided to replace him, although for me it was disappointing.

What was surprising was the arrival of Brian Clough; it was quite incredible that a man who had won the First Division title with Derby was now the manager of a club languishing in the lower reaches of the Third Division.

At the time he arrived I was quite looking forward to it because of the calibre of manager that he was, and what he'd already achieved in his career, let alone what he would go on to win. But on a personal basis his style of management didn't fit with me at all. Obviously with some players, like Tony Towner and the young centre-half Steve Piper it did. Those two boys came through it all and obviously matured under Brian Clough's type of management.

For the few months that Clough was in charge we were forever being tagged as 'Brian Clough's Brighton' and he loved the attention and the lime-light. But when we lost 8-2 at home to Bristol Rovers with half the pitch frozen and were knocked out of the FA Cup 0-4 at home in the first round by Walton & Hersham – a game I missed – he told us we were plain old Brighton & Hove Albion

It just didn't happen for me with Clough, despite being a virtual ever present in his side and scoring a dozen goals. I think I knew my time was up when I wasn't included on the end of season tour to Torremolinos. We're all grown men and there are ways of telling people that you're not part of their future plans. He could have told me face to face, but instead I discovered I'd been transfer listed when my neighbour told me he'd heard it on the radio.

Fortunately Gordon Lee came in for me at Blackburn, who were in what is now the Championship, and Brighton received a then club record fee of £26,000 for my services. Times certainly have changed!

I had two happy years at Blackburn, and went on to finish my career in the north west, with Bury and Port Vale, before returning to Tranmere and playing another fifty games for them.

I then took my coaching badge and joined Swindon as player-coach under manager John Trollope. When John left I was appointed manager in March 1983, but lasted just over a year. Lou Macari then replaced me. One success I had there was the signing of Garry Nelson, who went on to do great things with Brighton and later Charlton a few years later. He was a very decent player for me and I felt he should have gone on to play a far higher standard of football. It was nice to read some of the things he said about me in his book, *Left Foot Forward*. Like some of the Brighton players took to Clough, so he took to me as a manager.

I couldn't get another coaching job after I left Swindon and I was out of the game for two years before applying for the Commercial Manager's job at Blackburn. I am sure that having had a reasonable amount of success there as a player helped me get the job. I started there in October 1986 and have been there ever since.

In that time the game has changed immensely, of course. The club has also seen many changes. There were the fantastic Jack Walker years which culminated in us winning the title in 1994/95 and I've been privileged to work with some of the biggest names in football such as Kenny Dalglish, Roy Hodgson, the late Ray Harford and Graeme Souness.

But from a playing point of view, winning promotion at Brighton in 1972 was a big highlight and I'll never forget the game of my life against Rochdale all those years ago.

PETER WARD
FORWARD 1975-1980/1982-1983

BORN   27 July 1955
DEBUT   27 March 1976
ALBION CAREER   227 games, 95 goals

Peter Ward joined Albion for £4,000 in May 1975 from Burton Albion and after a year in the reserves went on to become one of the club's greatest goalscorers and one of the fans' all-time favourites. He scored 95 goals in 227 appearances for Brighton over two spells. His first coincided with the three greatest years in the club's history as Ward's goals helped lift Albion from the Third Division to the top flight, with promotion to the First Division clinched in Ward's match of his Albion life at Newcastle in May 1979.

Newcastle United 1 v Brighton & Hove Albion 3

League Division Two
Saturday 5 May 1979

St James' Park
Attendance 28,425

Ward is on target as the Seagulls win promotion to the top flight of
English football for the only time in the club's history

Teams

Bill McGarry	Manager	Alan Mullery
Kevin Carr	1	Eric Steele
Irving Nattrass	2	Chris Cattlin
Ken Mitchell	3	Gary Williams
(Sub. Gary Nicholson)		
Peter Manners	4	Brian Horton
David Barton	5	Andy Rollings
John Bird	6	Paul Clark
Alan Shoulder	7	Gerry Ryan
		(Sub. Malcolm Poskett)
Mick Martin	8	Peter Ward
Peter Withe	9	Teddy Maybank
Kenny Hibbitt	10	Peter Sayer
John Connolly	11	Peter O'Sullivan
Shoulder 80	Goals	Horton 12, Ward 25
		Ryan 43

Referee: G Nolan (Stockport)

I WAS NEVER AFFILIATED TO a league club as a youngster, and I got into the professional game through a more unorthodox route – although it was more common in the 1970s as clubs didn't have the extensive scouting networks and academy set ups which mean it is rare for a young boy to slip through the net these days. I was never spotted, perhaps it was because I was small, or perhaps I was a late developer, but I played boys and school football for fun and when I was a teenager signed for Borrowash Victoria, who played in the local Derby Combination.

I had left school and taken a job as an apprentice engine fitter at the Rolls Royce factory in Derby, which I combined with playing non-league football on a Saturday. I did very well for Borrowash and eventually came to the attention of Burton Albion – who played in the Southern League – and it was while I was with Burton that I first came to Brighton's attention. It was Brian Clough leaving Brighton that set the wheels in motion. Peter Taylor, who had always been Clough's right-hand man, decided against joining Clough at Leeds and stayed on at Brighton for a couple of seasons, stepping up from assistant as manager. Ken Guttridge, who had signed me at Burton, was recruited by Taylor to his coaching staff in 1974 and when he arrived, he told Taylor to sign me!

It was an on-off thing between Brighton and Burton – Taylor first bid for me late in 1974 and there was even talk of other players being involved in the deal – but it was decided I would stay at Burton until the end of the season. I know Brighton were keen for me to come during the season, but then it happened at the end of the season in May. I came down to the Goldstone Ground and had talks with Peter Taylor and then I signed. They could have offered me two pounds a week and I still would have signed, I just wanted to sign for a league club because I wanted to find out if I could make it as a professional player. It wasn't that I doubted myself, I just wasn't sure – especially being 20 years old as by then it was getting late really. I hadn't been with any league clubs at youth level and I had only played soccer locally.

It was a real shock going from part-time football to the pro game. The training was hard to start with, and I spent a year in the reserves. It wasn't until shortly before the end of the following season that I eventually got my chance in the first team – replacing respected top scorer Fred Binney in the side. I had been playing well in the reserves, scoring a few goals and they put me as sub for the first team. I was unused a couple of times – once at home and once at Bury – and then we went to Hereford. I had travelled with the team a few times, even when I wasn't a sub, so I wasn't expecting to be named in the side. I had a bout of flu the night before and coach and sponge man Glen Wilson filled me with whiskey. Peter had given Glen orders to give me the whiskey, but I just thought they were looking out for me because I was the sub, as we only had 12 players who had travelled. The next day we went for a walk and then had a team meeting and Peter just came out with it, "Fred you're out, Peter you're playing."

Things couldn't have worked out better as I scored after just 50 seconds of my debut and the game was shown on *Match of the Day*. In those days, there were only two or three games shown on the television on a Saturday evening, and having scored on my debut on *Match of the Day* it was unbelievable to discover what it meant. Everyone in the country knew who I was! That helped my confidence and I got more confident as games went along.

I finished the season with six goals in eight games and everything just seemed to go from there; things just all clicked into place. It was strange, in fact unbelievable, how everything slotted into place, particularly with the fans. I remember one occasion when my shorts got ripped – someone came in with a sliding tackle and tore my shorts with a tackle from behind, which of course were allowed in those days. The trainer brought out a new pair, and I changed my shorts right on the touchline in front of the West Stand and after hearing a few wolf whistles from the ladies, I wiggled my bum. They loved that, but it was just as though they had become my extended family.

When I had come into the side that season we were in the thick of the promotion shake up, but although I had ended the season strongly on a personal level, as a team we slipped up with three draws and a defeat in the final four games. At the end of that season Peter Taylor resigned as he felt he had failed by not winning promotion. He rejoined Clough, by then at Nottingham Forest, and went on to great glories on both domestic and European fronts. Our paths would cross again, but not before three or four glorious years with the Albion.

Alan Mullery came in and took over from Taylor and that proved an inspired appointment. We went up the following season and my goalscoring form continued. Everything I touched just seemed to turn to goals and I ended the season with 36 of them, which set a new club goals-in-a-season record which still stands today, but I didn't even know there was a record until I broke it! Unlike today – when the press and media are all over these sorts of things – nobody even mentioned it; not one of the other players, the manager, the media or the fans. Nobody told me I was just a few goals off the record. It was only when I actually beat it – I think at the end of the season – that I realised I had the record . . . and I didn't take all the penalties regularly. I only took them when Nobby Horton wasn't playing or he had missed, and I even recall Graham Cross taking one or two that season.

The next season not much was expected from us, but we had a good start – particularly in September when we went top of the old Second Division – and we stayed in and amongst the promotion sides throughout the campaign. We took it to the last game against Blackpool and I can remember that game really well. We needed to win and with our two nearest rivals Spurs and Southampton playing at the Dell, we needed one of the teams to win that game. We won our game: I scored the opener, before Nobby got a penalty in a 2-1 win, and I thought it was a great goal. It was one I will always remember and treasure. I remember thinking we were going up: right near the final whistle all the fans were going mad and celebrating and I thought that either Spurs or Southampton must have been winning – but then we found out at the final whistle it was 0-0 and that was a huge disappointment – but the following season was a fantastic ride.

We didn't have the best start in 1978/79, but we had an excellent run before Christmas, which lifted us into the promotion places. By February we were top of the table, and after an away defeat at Preston North End we only lost once, away at Cardiff, and went into a game at Newcastle on the final day of the season knowing a win would secure promotion and put us top of the table – although Crystal Palace still had one match left to play and so could nick the title from us.

We travelled up to the north east the Monday before the Newcastle game and we had quite a few days up there training and relaxing, mostly playing golf – although I was useless at golf back then. Alan Mullery was a very good manager. I liked him a lot and we had a great time together. Contrary to what has been said and written by others, things didn't go sour at the end, I think we just needed a break from one another having been together for so many years. He was a great manager, loyal to his players and he was very good in terms of his preparation.

About ten thousand Albion fans travelled to the Newcastle game. Everybody remembers the players celebrating in the sunshine at the final whistle, but those who were there will recall it snowed, it rained, it was sunny and it hailed. I think we had every bit of weather possible that afternoon – and that was at the beginning of May. Amazingly it was actually snowing during the game. The diversion of a strange weather system aside, it was one of the most nerve-wracking games I experienced. Newcastle were mid-table, with little to play for, but they were a good home team. They didn't often lose at St James' Park and we had to win to be sure we would go up.

Looking back now, having won 3-1, it seems like it was a quite straight-forward result, but it was actually not like that at the time. The pressure on us was huge – we were 90 minutes away from the club winning promotion to the top division for the first time in their history having missed out by a hair's breadth the previous season. But despite that pressure, we went out there and were unbelievable. Nobby Horton scored the opening goal with a header, while I netted the second goal and Gerry Ryan netted what you would have thought would be the clinching third.

We'd got three goals in the first half and while we were not thinking we had done it, we came in at half-time and were pretty pleased with ourselves. We were expecting Mullery to just say something along the lines of 'well done lads, keep it tight, more of the same' – but he went absolutely nuts. He had kept a lid on things all week, he'd not shown any signs of nervousness at all and I think it must have been all those pent up nerves coming out at once!

He must have been thinking, 'We're winning but if we blow it at this stage that would be an absolute nightmare.' I remember Nobby saying to him: "Gaffer! Calm down, relax, we are winning 3-0!" Nobby was a great skipper, he was brilliant, a very good captain – on and off the pitch. If I ever dropped back into my own half he would ask me what the hell I was doing and tell me to get back up front. He knew I couldn't defend to save my life and I could only go one way.

Another good character was Mark Lawrenson. He was great to have on your team and definitely one of the best players I have ever played with. He was pure class, world class. I played with him at Tampa Bay in the late 1980s, in fact it was him that got me to Tampa. He was a player coach for them after he had left Liverpool and his ill-fated spell as manager of Oxford

United. Lawro was unlucky as a manager, but it's great to see him making such a good career for himself with the BBC and other media. As a player he had all-round ability, although he never was a great goalscorer. He was good at the back, you could put him in midfield, he could head the ball well and he was a world-class all-round player.

Graham Moseley was another larger-than-life character. He and Eric Steele fought it out for the goalkeeper's shirt. You could have a good laugh with them two and both were important parts of that promotion-winning side.

Gerry Ryan was good character; a typical Irishman who made you laugh. I roomed with Gerry, so we saw a lot of each other. But everyone got on with each other. There was no thinking 'I don't like him'. We had a good rapport running through the squad, and all of the players got on extremely well. We had great team spirit and I think that always helps. We did all sorts of things together. We would go for a drink together. If there was a party everyone would be there – all together. That was important for us.

I can't say anything against Mullers, he was a great bloke, who I have the utmost respect for. He did, after all, manage the club to promotion into the top flight for the only time in its history.

Newcastle did pull one back in the second half, but as we got towards the final whistle, we were able to enjoy the last few moments of the game as we knew we were going up. It was a fantastic feeling when that final whistle blew and then the trip home from Newcastle was one big party. We travelled back by special train – the Pullman Brighton Belle – and with a huge number of supporters also on board the 12 coach train there was a lot of booze to be had. Up in first class, the directors, management and players cracked open champagne, but most of the way back to Brighton the players and fans were partying together. We always had a very special rapport with the supporters at Brighton. It would never happen today, a team having a celebratory booze up with its fans on the train on the way home, because it would be all over the papers and by the Monday morning there would be fines being dished out here, there and everywhere.

Incredibly when we arrived back into Brighton station, about 1 o'clock in the morning, there were thousands more supporters, who had not been able to travel up to Newcastle for the game, waiting for us to keep the party going!

We were rewarded for winning promotion with a trip to the United States of America. There was one sour note, though. When we were on the plane, the captain announced that our fiercest rivals, Crystal Palace, had won the league by beating Burnley in that game in hand to pip us to the title by one point.

The following season we kicked off in the First Division, but looking back it was the getting there that was the fun, that was unforgettable. We were in the bottom three for much of the early part of the season, but then we had a great run before Christmas – which we kicked off with a 1-0 win at the European champions Nottingham Forest in November and we eventually finished a very creditable 16th out of 22. I think even in the 20-team Premiership most newly promoted sides would accept a 16th-placed finish in their first full season in the top flight.

We began the following 1980/81 season quite well, but on a personal level my form wasn't great – largely because there was a lot of speculation that the club were going to sell me to Nottingham Forest, where Peter Taylor was now assisting Brian Clough. The on-off deal eventually went through in October 1980, and, although I had no desire to leave the club, I felt I could not turn down the chance of joining Nottingham Forest. They were European champions and I didn't regret going there because they were a great club.

After two years at Forest, I was given the chance to rejoin Brighton on loan. Alan Mullery, Brian Horton and Mark Lawrenson had all departed, but there were still plenty of familiar faces from my original spell: Graham Moseley, Steve Foster, Michael Robinson. Andy Ritchie was also there, the club had used the £400,000 they had received from Forest for me to sign Andy from Manchester United for half a million.

I remember the first game I played the gate was nine thousand up on the previous game, but my overriding memory from my second spell at Brighton was getting on and off aeroplanes! I was doing a lot of flying between East Midlands airport and Gatwick. I used to fly down from the Midlands on the Wednesday and then go back to Derby from wherever we played – unless we had two games in a week and then sometimes I would stay the whole week. I trained with Forest on the Monday and the Tuesday and then would train with Brighton the rest of the week.

I only scored a couple of league goals during my second spell – although one of those came in a 1-0 Goldstone win over my boyhood team Manchester United, a match I cherish for personal reasons almost as much as that win at Newcastle in 1979. And there was of course another famous Ward goal for Brighton at Newcastle, scored in the FA Cup third round replay in 1983. We had drawn with Newcastle at the Goldstone, but won the replay at St James' Park to set the club's famous cup run rolling. I played in both those Newcastle games and in the famous 2-1 win over Liverpool at Anfield in the fifth round, but I only played one more game for the club after that. Jimmy Melia and Brighton were keen to get me back on loan and I could have even played in the FA Cup final. I went and asked Brian Clough if he would let me go, but I can remember as clear as ever Cloughie saying to me in his famous voice: "Son. I've never played in a cup final... and neither will you!"

After that I opted to move to the US. I had been on loan at Seattle Sounders the previous summer and I moved on loan again – I remember watching the 1983 FA Cup final with my team-mates in a Seattle bar. I also had spells with Vancouver Whitecaps in Canada and Tampa Bay Rowdies, and until recently played veterans football, which is very well organised in America – but a knee operation has finally forced me to hang up my boots.

Nowadays I coach and run soccer camps in Tampa and details can be found at peterwardsoccer.com.

BRIAN HORTON
MIDFIELDER 1976–1981

BORN 4 February 1949
DEBUT 13 March 1976
ALBION CAREER 252 games, 41 goals

Brian Horton joined Albion from Port Vale in 1976 and was skipper for five of the most memorable years in the club's history as the side rose from the Third to the First Division. Hugely popular with Albion fans, he was even voted player of the season ahead of Peter Ward in 1976/77, the season in which Ward scored his record 36 goals in all competitions. Both players – Ward and Horton – selected Albion's victory at Newcastle United in May 1979, which clinched promotion to the top flight for the only time in the club's history.

Newcastle United 1 v Brighton & Hove Albion 3

League Division Two
Saturday 5 May 1979

St James' Park
Attendance 28,425

The Albion's popular and talismanic skipper leads the club to promotion to the First Division on one of the most memorable days in the club's history

Teams

Bill McGarry	Manager	Alan Mullery
Kevin Carr	1	Eric Steele
Irving Nattrass	2	Chris Cattlin
Ken Mitchell	3	Gary Williams
(Sub. Gary Nicholson)		
Peter Manners	4	Brian Horton
David Barton	5	Andy Rollings
John Bird	6	Paul Clark
Alan Shoulder	7	Gerry Ryan
		(Sub. Malcolm Poskett)
Mick Martin	8	Peter Ward
Peter Withe	9	Teddy Maybank
Kenny Hibbitt	10	Peter Sayer
John Connolly	11	Peter O'Sullivan
Shoulder 80	Goals	Horton 12, Ward 25
		Ryan 43

Referee: G Nolan (Stockport)

THE FIRST I HEARD of Brighton's interest in signing me was the day we went down to play at Crystal Palace for Port Vale in the old Third Division and I had heard that Palace, who were managed by Terry Venables at that time, were interested in signing me at the end of that season. I hadn't made my mind up at all and after the game, which we drew 2-2, the Port Vale manager Roy Sproson told me to get myself down to Brighton, as they were keen to sign me and the board had accepted a bid of £27,000 from Peter Taylor. I remember there was a Granada waiting outside Selhurst Park and it picked me up and whisked me straight down to Brighton that night. I had talks with the manager and he offered me a two-and-a-half-year deal, told me I would be captain and I signed for the club there and then – just before transfer deadline day. I didn't need to think twice.

I had played my final game for Port Vale at Palace on the Tuesday night, and I remember watching Brighton on the Wednesday evening against Shrewsbury Town. By half-time they were 2-0 down, but the team fought back with goals from Sammy Morgan and Fred Binney to maintain second place in the league. Three days later I was making my debut at Preston North End, but I actually only played 12 games under Peter Taylor, before he resigned at the end of the season after Brighton just missed out on promotion, finishing fourth behind Hereford, Cardiff and Millwall.

Taylor was replaced by Alan Mullery and I didn't know what to expect of him, but Alan turned out to be a fantastic manager and he had a huge influence on my career. I spoke to him recently – when Hull City played at Spurs in the Premiership – and he told me when he had taken the job at Brighton he had originally planned to come in as a player-manager, but once he took stock of his players at the club he felt I was a similar type of player and with me in the side there was no need for him to go out and play. That way he could concentrate on the management side of things.

We made a good start to the 1976/77 season under Mullers and we were up at the top of the Third Division for the whole of that campaign. There were some real stand-out games that year – non more so than a 7-0 win over Walsall – and we clinched promotion with a 3-2 win over Sheffield

Wednesday in front of a crowd of more than thirty thousand at the Goldstone. It was fantastic to win promotion in my first season, but we had been expected to do well as Brighton had a strong squad that had only just missed out under Peter Taylor the previous year.

We had some excellent players, Peter Ward obviously grabbed the plaudits with his 36 goals, but we had an excellent side from front to back: two great keepers in Peter Grummitt and Eric Steele, who came in for Peter during the run-in, Chris Cattlin, Andy Rollings, Graham Cross were all fantastic defenders, and Peter O'Sullivan was an excellent player. He'd begun his career with Manchester United and won international honours with Wales. He was a fine winger, but could also play inside. When he did play on the left wing, he gave us tremendous balance. Then there were the likes of Steve Piper, Tony Towner and Gerry Fell.

People had questioned me when I signed for Brighton, saying it wasn't a football town and asking me why was I going there – but to say Brighton wasn't a football town was nonsense to me. We were getting crowds of 34,000 and the Goldstone Ground was a fantastic place to play. There was a fantastic rapport between the players and fans during that era. That carried into the following season, when we were unlucky not to win promotion – and only missed out on the final day of the season when Southampton and Spurs played out a goalless draw to collect the point both sides needed for promotion. After that Alan Mullery promised we'd get promotion the next season. I think that was a bold statement, but I believe it helped us understand we were capable and some 12 months later we went into the final game of the season at Newcastle with our destiny in our own hands, not needing to rely on results elsewhere. That Newcastle game was the pinnacle of my career. I had played six years with Port Vale and two at Brighton in the lower leagues, so to finally win promotion to the top division – what is now the Premiership – was a marvellous achievement.

I remember Alan Mullery took us up to Newcastle a few days before the game and that was inspired management. The whole of Brighton was going crazy with promotion fever and Alan just took us away from it all and made us just relax for the week. We played a bit of golf, went to the pictures and hardly even trained that week. The manager felt that at that stage of the season we were more than fit enough after a long and hard campaign. Again, that was excellent management and it took a huge amount of pressure off of us ahead of the biggest game in the club's history. We took the lead on the day, when I got my head on a corner, Peter Ward got a second and Gerry Ryan put the result beyond doubt. It's well documented that Alan Mullery went mad at the break – but I think it was just the pressure of the day. Newcastle came back at us, but the final whistle signalled the start of the celebrations. Then came the train ride home, and on the Sunday we all went to Harry Bloom's hotel for lunch, and had an open-top bus ride around the town.

We had a very tough start to life in the First Division, getting hammered 4-0 by Arsenal at the Goldstone in the opening game, but we eventually found our feet and adjusted to life in the top division. The following season we stayed up too – but that wasn't quite as straightforward. We lost at Middlesbrough and were bottom of the table with four games left to play and everybody was writing us off and telling us we were going to be relegated. But we then won 3-0 at Crystal Palace, beat Leicester City at the Goldstone and won at Sunderland, 2-1. That meant if we beat Leeds at the Goldstone Ground, on the final day, we would stay up. We won 2-0, thanks to goals from Steve Foster and Andy Ritchie, and that proved to be my last game for the club – although I didn't realise it at the time – but strangely Eva Petulengro, the famous astrologist and clairvoyant who read palms and told fortunes on Brighton Pier, had predicted it!

Some years earlier I had been asked along to a pub opening, it was the uncle of Eric Steele who was opening the pub, and as part of the evening's entertainment Eva Petulengro told my fortune. She had all the cards and the crystal ball and it was during our first season in the Second Division and she correctly predicted we would go close to promotion that season – but narrowly miss out – but then win promotion the following campaign. Amazingly she was right, as we missed out on the final day – we beat Blackpool, but Spurs and Southampton drew, which meant they both went up in the second and third positions and we finished fourth, just outside the three automatic spots. That was a huge disappointment, but true to Eva's amazing prediction we went up the following season.

It had all been in the papers, I think it was *The Sun* and the local paper and then Eva contacted me again during my final season with the club and asked if I would have my fortune told again – it was only ever the football which she looked at – and I agreed. I remember John Vinnicombe from the *Evening Argus* came along with me as he wanted to write a piece for the paper. I remember Eva looking into her crystal ball and saying, "Bad news Brian!" She then proceeded to tell me Brighton would be relegated at the end of that season – but even worse still both myself and Alan Mullery would leave the club at that point too. I called Alan straight away, still in the company of *Argus* man John, and asked him what I should do, could the papers print it – but Alan being as he was just said, "It's fine. Let them print it!"

I didn't give it much thought after that even when with four games to go, we looked dead and buried. A superb four-game winning sequence saved us. Although Eva was wrong about the club suffering relegation, and she was only just wrong, she was eventually proved right on her predicition that Alan and I would be leaving the club, as Alan handed in his resignation and it wasn't long before I followed him out of the Goldstone.

It had all come to a head over Mark Lawrenson's proposed transfer away from Brighton – and while it wasn't an issue that Mark was leaving, everyone accepted he was a class player, capable of playing at the very highest level, there was a split over where he went. Alan had done a deal with Ron Atkinson at Manchester United to sell Mark for £900,000 – but quite separately the board of directors had agreed to sell Mark to Liverpool for the same price. It might seem insignificant, but Alan felt he had been undermined and matters came to a head and it all ended with Alan resigning from his post at the club during a meeting with the board, aimed to clear the air.

I lived opposite Hove Park at the time, and I remember Alan knocking on my door out of the blue one evening. It was immediately after that meeting and he told me he had just handed in his resignation and was leaving the club. I was shocked, but then he dropped another bombshell when he told me the club wanted to sell me to Luton and advised me that I should go! I didn't know what to do, so I went in to meet the new manager Mike Bailey, who told me at the age of 31 I would have to prove myself all over again. I wasn't impressed, and I remember telling him I had nothing to prove at Brighton – either to him, the fans or anyone else. I also told him that he was the only one who had something to prove. After that I felt it was time to move on and signed for Luton and linked up with David Pleat, who was a great coach.

I had some fantastic times during three years with Luton as we won promotion in my first season there and then we stayed in the top division, and the season Brighton got relegated from the First Division we beat them 5-0 at Kenilworth Road early on in that campaign and I felt that result and performance proved Bailey wrong. We beat Brighton again 4-2 at the Goldstone later on that season – but by that time Bailey had departed. Of course I did not want to see Brighton go down, but those two wins were extremely satisfying, not because it was Brighton – they were the last team and set of fans I wanted to inflict that on – but because it proved Mike Bailey wrong.

After Luton I moved into management with Hull City, where I took the job as player-manager. The club were in the old Third Division and we won promotion to the Second Division in my first full season. Over the next three years we were never in trouble in the second tier, and we even went close to promotion to the First Division in one season – which was Hull's best-ever finish until last season – and I became a director of the club. I think I am still the only ever player, manager and director of a club. However in 1988 the chairman decided it was time for me to go, but I felt that was a very unfair sacking – and within an hour of sacking me, I had him on the phone asking me to go back because he knew he had made a mistake. The players had kicked up a fuss, but I felt it was time to move on and decided against it and joined Oxford United as Mark Lawrenson's assistant. After Mark left, I took the manager's job and worked with Kevin Maxwell, who proved to be a fantastic chairman, because he just let me get on with managing the team. From there I was lucky enough to be headhunted by Manchester City in August 1993, which was a fantastic opportunity to go and manage in the First Division and I felt I did a good job at Maine Road, building a very good side, which was on the verge of good things but I got the sack at the end of the 1994/95 season – again unfairly in my opinion – although there had been a change of Chairman and Francis Lee wanted to appoint his good friend Alan Ball as manager.

I felt we were very close to being a very good top-flight side, and with hindsight, I would imagine Francis Lee would view his decision to sack me as a mistake, as the following season City were relegated. It took them a long time to fully recover from that, as they slipped down through the leagues. I think City fans appreciated what I did there. Certainly I have always been warmly welcomed back there by fans and staff at the club.

After City, I took a job at Huddersfield and very nearly got them to the First Division playoffs, with a shot at the Premiership – but we suffered from injuries, and I felt we were unfortunate, but that didn't stop the chairman deciding it was time to change the manager. I had around a year out of the game, and then Dick Knight – for whom I have a huge amount of respect – offered me the opportunity to come back to Brighton as manager in February 1998. The club was at an all-time low. The ground had been sold and even though Dick had come in the club was still in a terrible state and needed a lot work. The first team were down the bottom of the Third Division, the reserves were bottom and the youth team were bottom – but I could see amidst all that doom and gloom that they had some fantastic people at the club, who were keeping them going through those dark days; such as Derek Allan the club secretary, Sally Townsend, who held things together in the office, and Malcolm Stuart the physio. I had Jeff Wood on my staff – who was a brilliant number two – and we stabilised things and kept the club up that season.

That summer Dick asked me to stay on and take things forward and I agreed to another 12 months – but it wasn't easy with the club playing at Gillingham, the training ground at the University of Sussex and no permanent offices. That made things extremely difficult, but I think we had a good go at things and, when I left, the club were in a play-off place in the Third Division. That was a very difficult decision – one of the toughest I have had to make in my career. Had Brighton been playing at the Goldstone – or possibly even Withdean – I would never have left. I then had five good years at Port Vale, we got to the Millennium and won the LDV Final in 2001 – but I decided it was time to go when the old chairman left in 2004 and a supporters' group came in to run the club. I couldn't work with them and found it very difficult and felt I didn't have much choice but to go.

From there I went to Macclesfield. I went there when they were bottom of the league and looking doomed with seven games to go but we managed to keep them up. The following season I took them into the play-offs and to the northern area final of the LDV, but we lost to Carlisle on away goals. I should really have left at the end of that season – and with hindsight I made a mistake staying on. I had the opportunity to go to Carlisle in the summer of 2006, when Paul Simpson left Brunton Park – and I should have left for Carlisle then – but I stayed with Macclesfield Town, which was always a difficult job as I had the smallest budget in the Football League, and I ended up parting company with the club in October 2006. I'm proud of my achievements as a manager, I had 22 years in management and was in charge for over 1,000 games – and there are only 13 other bosses who have achieved that in English football.

I had a spell out of the game, but I remember Phil Brown – someone I had not worked with previously – contacting me while he was caretaker-boss at Hull and asking me if I had ever considered going with a younger manager. Then when he had kept Hull up in the Championship and got the job permanently he asked me to go in as his assistant – and it was fantastic to go back to Hull, where I already had a good rapport with the club and the fans.

Phil doesn't treat me like a number two, I am more like an advisor to him than a traditional number two. I take a more objective view of games; I sit in the stand and have a headset on, linked into Phil in the dugout. I still get out on the training ground every day, which is the best bit, as I love the banter. I love it. Anyone who knows me knows my passion for the game and it is as strong as ever.

I am thoroughly enjoying my second spell at Hull, especially with the way we have played and achieved results in the club's first ever season in the Premier League, and I am not sure if I would go back into management. Mind you, you don't know until you get the offer – and I don't think Phil would stand in my way – but as I found out with Brighton for the first time all those years ago, the top flight is definitely the place to be.

GARY WILLIAMS
FULL-BACK 1977–1982

BORN   8 March 1954
DEBUT   13 August 1977
ALBION CAREER   177 games, 8 goals

Gary Williams joined Albion from Preston North End. A cultured attacking full-back, he was blessed with a fierce shot and loved to get forward. A popular figure with the Albion fans, he had the uncanny knack of coming up with important goals at vital times . . . none more important than his vital strike at Sunderland in 1981 which went a long way to helping Albion ensure their top-flight survival.

Sunderland 1 v Brighton & Hove Albion 2

League Division One
Saturday 25 April 1981

Roker Park
Attendance 22,317

Williams scores a great goal to set the Albion on their
way to top-flight survival

Teams

	Managers	
Ken Knighton		Alan Mullery
Barry Siddall	1	Perry Dogweed
Joe Hinnigan	2	Chris Ramsey
Joe Bolton	3	Gary Williams
Rob Hindmarch	4	Brian Horton
Shaun Elliott	5	Steve Foster
Gary Rowell	6	Mark Lawrenson
Gordon Chisholm	7	John Gregory
Mike Buckley	8	Andy Ritchie
		(Sub. Gerry Ryan)
Tom Ritchie	9	Michael Robinson
Alan Brown	10	Gordon Smith
(Sub. Rafael Maranon)		
Stan Cummins	11	Peter O'Sullivan
Brown 62	Goals	Robinson 36, Williams 89

Referee: J Worrall (Warrington)

I FIRST CAME TO BRIGHTON'S notice when I was playing for Preston North End. The two clubs were in the same division, the Third, and it was season 1976/77 when I first heard of their interest. The Albion were having quite a good season. In those days, before the introduction of the play-offs, only the top three teams went up at the end of the season, so there were usually only about four or five teams involved in the promotion race. At the time Brighton were one of them, and I remember thinking they were one of the teams to beat. Preston too were in with a chance of promotion, although we had got beaten 2-0 at the Goldstone that season. I think I might have impressed the manager Alan Mullery that day, but the player that impressed him most was a young lad called Mark Lawrenson and as a result there was a six or seven month period when Brighton had scouts going and watching Preston, mainly to watch Mark and to see how good he was. That can't have done me any harm as it turned out, as they saw plenty of me as well.

Preston missed out on promotion, although we tried our best at North End, but we fell just short, finishing sixth. We missed out by only five points, but Mark and I ended up in the Second Division when we both joined Brighton. Obviously Alan Mullery had gone to watch a few Preston games and, as well as being struck by Mark being an excellent player, also took a fancy to the left-back as well! In fact I had won Preston's Player of the Season trophy in the previous season, while Mark won it in that 76/77 campaign.

A lot of people still say to this day that we came down from Preston together, but it wasn't quite like that. It was in the papers at the end of that season that Brighton were interested in Mark Lawrenson, who was only 20 at the time. In fact a lot of clubs were. We were actually away on holiday together – we were pretty close at Preston – and he had to leave the holiday early after he received the phone call from the chairman of North End asking him to come back as there was a deal going on.

Subsequently we read all about it in the newspapers and found out he had signed for Brighton for the eye-catching fee of £111,111.

Two or three weeks later my phone rang and the caller said, "Hi Gary, it's Alan Mullery." I didn't believe it, though. I thought, 'I'm not having this. It's one of my mates taking the Mickey.' But when he said, "Get the next train down to Brighton and we'll have a discussion if you're interested," I realised I was talking to the real Alan Mullery! I just said, "Yes, I'd love to come down and have chat with you . . . but are you going to pay for the train fare?"

I wasn't on a lot of money in those days and I knew it was a long way down to Brighton from Preston and I began to panic.

"Where am I going to stay?" I asked.

Alan reassured me by telling me, "don't worry. You just get your arse down here, we'll pay for your expenses."

The club put me up at the Metropole and I didn't sign the first day because I was trying to be clever after the club made me an offer on wages. We didn't have agents in those days and I was a very young 21 and I was going on the advice my mates back home had been telling me: try and hold out.

"I'll have to think about it!" I said, but even before I'd spoken to a few friends back in Preston to discuss the offer on the table, I looked out the balcony – it was a clever trick by the club, putting me in that room overlooking the sea – and it was a lovely evening. I remember there were lots of people out skateboarding along the seafront – and I looked out over the famous beach and thought, 'this isn't a bad place to be'.

I think my stalling tactic managed to get me an extra £20 a week – which was better than nothing, but looking back we weren't exactly paid great wages. Mullery said to me that the club was taking a chance, and I had prove myself. I remember him saying, "look, this is a great club. Look at the crowds, we're going places."

He was right. Brighton were now in the old Second Division and in those days the Goldstone was housing the biggest crowds in the country outside the First Division. The catchment area was fantastic, the supporters were brilliant and with a 28,000 fan base, I thought to myself that I would regret turning down a move to Brighton. At that time it was a great club to join.

We won promotion to the top flight in my second season, 1978/79, but the first season still stands out as one people remember as we came so close to going up. That campaign we were in a four-horse promotion race with Bolton, Spurs and Southampton; the four of us were about ten points clear of everybody else. It was a four-horse race, although if you believed the papers then Bolton, Southampton and Spurs were as good as up. The so-called experts didn't think we could maintain our challenge until the end of the season, but we did. Spurs came down to the Goldstone and we hammered them 3-1. The game was interrupted by a pitch invasion by disgruntled Tottenham fans, which was well documented in the media. They were great days, you would have 30,000 inside the ground and more locked out, and the Goldstone had an electric atmosphere.

Despite the media's doubts, it all came down to the last game. Bolton were up, but we played Blackpool at home, while Spurs and Southampton played each other knowing that a point would be enough for both sides, and would freeze us out of the promotion picture. The fans all had their ears glued to radios, like it is on the last game of every season. We just focused on getting the win, but I think deep down everybody expected Spurs would go to Southampton and draw. There was a lot of talk about conspiracy theories, but I don't think that was the case. We missed out on the goal difference. There were tears everywhere and then came the famous statement from Mullery when he told the fans from the West Stand not to worry as we would definitely go up the next year.

We fancied ourselves, but it was a bold statement and it meant a lot of pressure was on the players (and the manager) when we started the next season. We were gutted we had missed out, but we thought that having come so close, with an additional couple of new signings, a good manager behind us and a great set of lads, we had as good a chance as any other side. We weren't cocky, but we had a grit and determination. We were beaten in the second game of the season, 2-0 at home to Cambridge United, although we had battered them, they somehow nicked the win, but the *Evening Argus* sports pages were already telling us we could only afford six more slip ups all season. Apparently we could only afford to get beaten seven times in a season and still have a chance of promotion – as it transpired we lost nine games.

We played Newcastle United at St James' Park in the last game of the season, knowing victory would seal our promotion to the top flight – for the first time in the club's history. Mullery decided he had to take us away from town because the atmosphere was building up so much, even with a week to go. Everyone was talking about the game. The numbers going were crazy, about ten thousand Albion fans made the journey up to Newcastle . . . and that's not counting some who never made it all the way! I later learned that some of them took three weeks to get back. Mullery took us out of town five days before the game and we watched Newcastle in a midweek fixture, and we were relaxed a bit because it was before mobile telephones, and we didn't have people ringing us up asking for tickets, this that and the other. It all now boiled down to the 90 minutes and we had the added pressure of expectation as our fate was in our own hands, something we hadn't had the year before.

We came good on the day and played some fantastic football as we really blew Newcastle away to lead 3-0 at half-time. I wouldn't have fancied it being 0-0 at half-time because it doesn't matter how good a player you are that pressure of possibly losing nine months of hard work would have been mind-blowing. I wouldn't even have been comfortable at 2-0, because if Newcastle had got a goal back that could have caused panic – so 3-0 was a good score for us.

But you wouldn't have believed it if you had been in the Albion dressing room at half-time. There was the loudest row anyone's ever heard – even afterwards in the players lounge the Newcastle players asked what was going on, even though they were 3-0 down and getting a roasting off their own manager they'd heard the ruckus coming from our dressing room next door. I remember we were at each others' throats because we still felt under pressure being so close to the biggest achievement ever for the club and for all of us personally.

I still think we'd played really well, but Mullery went mad at us. Someone had gone through one-on-one with our keeper, and one of our defenders hadn't covered. Someone hadn't picked up one of their players. I think it might even have been me! He lost it and of course even 3-0 up, we still felt under a lot of pressure, because we could blow a season's work in 45 minutes. We were all going a bit crazy, but it was because we were on adrenaline, the nerves were kicking in.

Newcastle did pull one back in the second half, but when the final whistle eventually blew the feeling was fantastic. It was one of the best moments of my career. It was the only time I won promotion, and I never suffered relegation, so I guess that is what stands out on my CV – but that was at a time when there were no play-offs and you had to be in the top three to get promoted, which for me makes it that bit more special. When the final whistle went to end the game and our season the relief was fantastic. The emotion and the adulation from the crowd was incredible.

The next day we did a coach trip round the town and just the whole thing was amazing. Looking back now, I still get a buzz just thinking about it.

The next season things didn't start so well, but we turned things around. I remember we did the double over Nottingham Forest, who were European Champions, and I scored the winner at the Goldstone Ground. People always remember that goal against Forest. Fans still come up to me now and say 'I was there' – the amount of people who have said that to me means there must have been at least 48,000 fans at the Goldstone that night! But they still come up to me and say, "I was stood right behind it and I saw it go in!" It's become sort of a legend. Everytime I talk about that goal it gets even better, so now I always say I picked up the ball in Hove Park and kicked it and it just went in at the other end! I just make it up as I go along!

Joking aside, that goal was extra special because it was against the reigning European Champions. They were one of the biggest teams in Europe and we had beaten them at their place and then at the Goldstone to do the double over them. I guess the whole thing was fate really. These things sometimes happen, you give it your best shot and just sometimes it works out for you.

After surviving by six points in our first season in the top flight, it was a similar story in the 1980/81 season, but whereas we were fairly safe as we came towards the end of our first season, we were struggling in 1981 after a really bad run in March. With four games left to play we looked dead and buried. We needed to win all four games to have any realistic chance of staying up – but we managed it to pull off the great escape.

I remember the meeting we had before those four games, and Alan Mullery has to take the credit for it. He had all the squad there and he said to us, "this is a showdown. We've got four games left and we have to win them all – otherwise I am going to get the sack!" It was a fairly aggressive meeting, he could be like that, and he said something like, "if you don't do it, if you don't win all these four games and you get me the sack, if I see you on the street or if I see you out I will run you over, I will kill you!"

He got himself into this frenzy and instilled a do-or-die mentality. There was no try and keep it tight, try and do this and do that. It was just get out there and do it. We went to Palace – they were struggling too – but we hammered them 3-0. That gave us a bit of momentum and we won our next game, at the Goldstone against Leicester City by 2-1. Then we faced Sunderland, they were down there with us, and we knew that if we didn't win we could be relegated that afternoon at Roker Park.

We took the lead 1-0, but Sunderland pegged us back – and we were playing for our lives. We knew if results went against us elsewhere even a draw might see us relegated – but with virtually the last kick of the game I

got the winner. It was one of the most important goals I scored for the
Albion as it was such a vital win. The fact was that we stayed up by two
points that season, so perhaps that means that was the most important goal
I scored for the Albion although the goal that is always remembered is the
one against Nottingham Forest, perhaps because it was at the Goldstone.

We had flown up to Sunderland for that game and I remember when we
landed at Gatwick we had a coach there to pick us up – but being the hero,
I got collared by the local radio station to do an interview. I felt on cloud
nine, but I had the wind taken out of my sails when I finished the interview
when I discovered that the lads had got on the coach and already left! I was
stranded. Luckily there was an Albion supporter, a chap named Danny
Hornby, who had come up to the airport to meet the lads who was still
there and he gave me a lift home to Brighton.

We won our final game of the season, 2-0 against Leeds United, and that
ensured our survival – but then that summer we lost some key individuals
at the club with the manager leaving and our star players moving on. The
biggest loss at the end of the season was Mullery, but we also lost Mark
Lawrenson. Mark was a great player, but I felt we could have lived without
him – I thought Alan Mullery was always very shrewd in the transfer
market and would have found a replacement – but losing the manager was
bad because he held us all together. In my opinion, though the biggest loss
of all was our skipper Brian Horton. He was our manager as far as the
players were concerned when we were out there on the pitch; he was our
leader and it took the heart away from our side when he left to go to Luton.
He was one of the best players who ever played for Brighton, not just
because he was an excellent holding midfielder, but Nobby would hold the
side together when we were struggling. He used to get you pumped up,
he'd get in your face, shouting at his own players when things weren't going
well, and he would get at the opposition. He was a total warrior, a real team
player and club man, he would help you off the pitch as well. He was a great
friend and he was always organising get-togethers for the boys: we would
go out for meals with the wives, or be out playing golf. We were a close-knit
family and Nobby was a huge part of all that. And of course he was a hell
of a player.

You can actually see – if you know your stuff – who's running the dressing room. Mullery was the manager, but he had a great right-hand man in
Nobby, a general on the pitch and in the dressing room. It's often the way
that the centre-forward gets the man-of-the-match award because he scored

four goals but the player who has done all the work will be that midfield man. Basically Nobby was the man pulling all strings and controlling the team. We might be trailing 1-0 away from home in a hostile atmosphere and he was the one, in the trenches if you like, battling away. Somehow we'd turn things around and get a draw or even nick a win. We missed something when he wasn't playing, more so than if Mark Lawrenson was missing. Mark was a world-class defender, but when the question comes up, who was the best player ever at Brighton?

For the club, in terms of what he brought to the team, I always say Nobby was the top man. Similarly when it comes to managers, when you see what Alan Mullery achieved while at the Albion, for me he was the best-ever manager and I was lucky to play under him in that team which was promoted up to what is now the Premiership from the old Third Division. That was one hell of an achievement. Mullery has got to take a lot of credit for that, but he had the right chairman and he had some decent players – although he acquired plenty of them himself, of course.

Even now you see Alan on *Sky Sports* and he still talks well – but I've seen him at close hand with shards of glass in his hand having smashed a glass or something, telling us to give more effort and he can be frightening.

Before that Sunderland game he was great. He knew we were nervous and just as he had when we went to Newcastle, he took us away to play some golf. We went to a town in the middle of nowhere, and he was laughing and joking and keeping things light-hearted. Alan was great because he didn't let us worry about things. He made us concentrate on what we had to do and we were successful that way.

We were an all-out attacking team but all this changed when the new manager Mike Bailey came in. I remember one team talk Alan gave when the opposition came down and they were staying in the same hotel as us. They walked past us a couple of times and Alan Mullery said, "I haven't got a team talk today . . . but did you see their faces when they walked past us? They were petrified!" That was the sort of thing he did; he could change your state of mind with one comment and we went away feeling confident about winning and motivated. It was that sort of thing that kept us going, that's why I thought he was the top man.

Mullery leaving was the beginning of the end for me at Brighton, as my style of play didn't really suit the new manager. I was encouraged to attack under Alan Mullery, but we became much more defensive and that wasn't my style. I eventually moved on to Crystal Palace, however I moved back to Brighton when I ended my playing career and now run my own business here. I do look out for the results and consider myself an Albion fan and try and get along to Withdean when I can, but it's never easy getting tickets. It will be great when the club finally gets the new stadium . . . then who knows, they might be able to repeat those glorious feats of the late 1970s and early 1980s.

Gary has dedicated his chapter in Match Of My Life to his two children, Ben and Grace.

STEVE FOSTER
CENTRE-HALF 1979–1984/1992-96

BORN   24 September 1957
DEBUT   28 August 1979
ALBION CAREER   332 games, 15 goals

Steve Foster joined Brighton from Portsmouth for £150,000. At Fratton he'd begun life as a centre-forward, but ended up forging a hugely successful career at centre-half after being employed in the position as an emergency for Pompey. After Brighton, he played for Aston Villa, Luton Town and Oxford United before returning to the Goldstone under Barry Lloyd in 1992. Steve, who wore a distinctive headband on his head to keep his locks under control, is also one of only three players to be capped by England whilst at Albion. He also skippered the club during the famous 1983 FA Cup run, and it's the semi-final which he selects as the Albion match of his life.

Brighton & Hove Albion 2 v Sheffield Wednesday 1

FA Cup semi-final
Saturday 16 April 1983

Highbury
Attendance 54,627

*Case and Robinson score the goals which take the Albion
to Wembley for the very first time*

Teams

Jimmy Melia	Managers	Jack Charlton
Graham Moseley	1	Bob Bolder
Gary Stevens	2	Mel Sterland
Graham Pearce	3	Pat Heard
Tony Grealish	4	Mark Smith
Steve Foster	5	Mick Lyons
Steve Gatting	6	Gary Shelton
Jimmy Case	7	Gary Megson
Gary Howlett	8	Simon Mills
Michael Robinson	9	Gary Bannister
Gordon Smith	10	Ian McCulloch
Neil Smillie	11	Ante Mirocevic
Case 51, Robinson 78	Goals	Mirocevic 57

Referee: G Courtney (Spennymoor)

I ARRIVED AT BRIGHTON FOR MY first spell with the Albion in 1979 when the club had just been promoted to the First Division, so quite obviously there was a real buzz around the whole town. Being just along the coast at Portsmouth, I was quite aware of Brighton's achievements over the preceding three years and jumped at the opportunity to join a club who were on the up. I was a few weeks short of my 22nd birthday when Alan Mullery signed me and it was a big step up from the Third Division. There was also quite a hefty fee involved. It sounds small today, but back then £150,000 was a fairly big amount for a third-flight defender.

I wasn't involved in the opening game of the season, at home to Arsenal, and it was a baptism of fire for the club as we lost the first three games against the Gunners, Aston Villa and Manchester City quite heavily. In those days there was only one substitute too, so I hadn't even been involved in a squad, but Mullery called me into the side for my debut against Cambridge United in the League Cup. I kept my place for the next league game, against Bolton Wanderers at the Goldstone Ground and that kicked off a little run for us as we only lost once, at Spurs, over an eight-game spell. However, that 2-1 defeat at White Hart Lane also saw us lose my defensive partner Mark Lawrenson to injury. We didn't have a big squad so Gary Stevens came in from the youth team and did really well. In fact he did so well that when Mark Lawrenson returned to fitness, Alan Mullery was able to push him into midfield; something he also did with John Gregory, who could operate at the back or in the middle.

Despite our good run in September, October was a bad month as we faced a trip to Manchester United, the return game with Arsenal, and in early November we entertained Liverpool at the Goldstone. We lost all three games, and slipped up against Coventry and Norwich. I scored my first goal for the club against the Canaries in that game at the Goldstone, but the 4-2 defeat saw us sink to the bottom of the table, and I would have swapped my goal for maximum points. Our only point in October came from a goalless draw against Leeds United, and when we travelled to

Nottingham to face Forest, the reigning European Champions, on Saturday 17th November, we were 21st in the table, and being one of the new clubs of the division many people, as often happens with sides who come up, had written us off as relegation certainties.

The trip to Nottingham coincided with Mark Lawrenson's return from injury and the arrival of experienced defender Peter Suddaby, who had joined on a free transfer from Blackpool. With Mark playing in midfield and Peter lining up at right-back, we pulled off one of the finest results in the club's history – beating the champions of Europe in the their own back-yard. Gerry Ryan got the goal early in the game, and Forest really came at us in search of the equaliser, but we held firm and that result gave us the confidence going forward.

We drew our next game, away at Middlesbrough, beat Derby at the Goldstone and then lost at Everton, before going on a tremendous run through Christmas and on into the New Year. We won five and drew two in the next seven games, including a 3-0 win over fierce rivals Crystal Palace and a thumping 4-1 win over Manchester City – in front of the TV cameras at the Goldstone Ground. Defeats to Tottenham and Southampton were followed by a bizarre sequence of six straight draws, but by that time we were starting to breathe much easier as we had a bit of space between ourselves and the relegation places. We eventually finished the season seven points clear of the drop zone, but not before completing a double over Forest, by repeating our 1-0 win at the Goldstone, thanks to an absolutely stunning goal from Gary Williams.

The following season was another long, hard – but ultimately successful – battle against the drop. We looked dead and buried at one point, with four matches to play, but a maximum eight points from those last four games ensured we would be in the top flight for another season. A huge factor that year was striker Michael Robinson, who Alan Mullery had signed the previous summer from Manchester City for a fairly sizeable fee of £400,000. That was a lot of money for a club of Brighton's size, even as a top-flight team, but it proved money extremely well spent as Robbo was a brilliant player for the club and he weighed in with a very good total of 22 goals in all competitions that season. Gordon Smith was another very good player who had arrived the previous season – and he also finished with double figures, scoring 10 times in the First Division in a season in which he played mostly as a midfielder.

Peter Ward left during the October, signing for Nottingham Forest, and Andy Ritchie joined from Manchester United for a club record fee of

£500,000. Andy took a little while to settle, but he too weighed in with vital goals that season.

Michael Robinson and Gordon Smith spearheaded our run to Wembley in 1983, but not before some managerial upheaval at the club. Alan Mullery left at the end of the 1980/81 season, and was replaced by Mike Bailey. A few of the club's heroes from the promotion push also departed, players who had served the club well for a number of years. Bailey got off to an excellent start as manager, and midway through the 1981/82 season we were up amongst the top six, previously uncharted territory. Mike Bailey's tactics were based on a solid defence, the cornerstone for any good team, but it wasn't popular with a section of the supporters and media and by December 1982, despite bringing fans' favourite Peter Ward back to the club on loan, Mike was sacked. The club were hovering just above the relegation places when George Aitken and Jimmy Melia took over.

The next five months would be amongst the most memorable in the club's history as we embarked on the club's greatest-ever cup run. Who would have thought after a 1-1 draw against Second Division Newcastle United at the Goldstone Ground that we would end our run at Wembley, against Manchester United?

I was suspended for the replay up in the north east. We beat Newcastle at St James' Park, with Wardy netting the winning goal on Tyneside – although the team did survive a couple of scares in the closing minutes of the game. Newcastle threw everything at the boys, and had two attempts ruled out for offside on the night, but our lads held on for the win to set up a home fourth round tie with Manchester City.

I was back in the team for the Manchester City match and that was one of our best performances of the season. It underlined what we were capable of, but we just couldn't find a level of consistency that season. We cruised past City with ease, smashing four past them: Jimmy Case and Neil Smillie were on target with one apiece and Michael Robinson got a brace, which he really enjoyed, being against his former team. City were down the bottom of the table with us and were eventually relegated too, but that cup defeat was the final straw for John Bond – who quit Maine Road on the Monday after that defeat.

Our reward for the win was a fifth round trip to Liverpool – and from that round on we got the draws we wanted. At that stage we wanted the big draw, the trip to Anfield, the opportunity to play on the big stage. I didn't realise at the time, but we were 9/1 to win that game and 80/1 to win the FA Cup outright. The 9/1 price was an astonishing one given that this was a two horse race we were talking about, but it also puts the game into perspective and in particular the chance the rest of the football world gave us of coming away from Anfield with the win – but we did!

The game was played on a Sunday, because Everton had also been drawn at home and had played against Spurs on the previous day. We got off to a great start when Gerry Ryan scored after about half an hour – silencing the Kop in the process – and although they found their voices when Craig Johnston levelled the scores with about 20 minutes of the game left to play, we went straight down the other end and Jimmy Case, a former Red, fired a brilliant winner. Jim was a keen Liverpool supporter, and had followed the club as a teenager, while he was playing part-time and working as a labourer. He then played for the Reds through some glorious years, winning the European Cup and League Championship amongst other honours. I think that goal meant an awful lot to him. He stayed up on Merseyside with his family – all keen Reds – after the game, and I remember him telling us, when he got back to Brighton, that he went home that night, only to find his family had moved the key from its usual hiding place so he couldn't get in!

Victory at Anfield made a few people sit up and take notice – and when we were drawn at home to Norwich City, our odds tumbled and we felt we had a real chance of going all the way to the final. Jimmy scored again that day and that was one of the greatest days the Goldstone has ever hosted. There were 28,800 packed in and it made for a brilliant atmosphere inside the old ground. The 1-0 win put us into the semi-final, but also landed Jimmy Melia the manager's job on a permanent basis. To win at Anfield was special for Jimmy as well a he had been a player at the club when Bill Shankly had arrive and revolutionised the place.

When it came to the semi-final draw, once again we all got our wish when we avoided both Arsenal and Manchester United. All we wanted now was to get to Wembley and we found ourselves drawn against the winner of the all Second Division quarter-final replay between Burnley and Sheffield Wednesday. A 5-0 replay win meant it was Wednesday, at Highbury, who stood between the Albion and a place in the 1983 FA Cup Final.

Sheffield Wednesday were a good side, boasting the likes of Bob Bolder in goal, Mel Sterland in defence, Gary Megson in midfield and Gary Bannister up front. I remember we lost the toss to wear the blue and white stripes so we were playing in our yellow change kit.

I don't really recall any of the actual play in the semi-final match, but I can recall the goals. When you play in any game your focus is on what you have to do and then it is gone in a flash, I rarely remember details or specific incidents. It is only the games I have been able to watch again on video that have allowed the memories to come back, but without that prompt I have never been one to remember much detail. Little things stand out, though, I remember Graham Moseley getting kicked during the game, and now I've seen it I can remember my clearance off the line.

Thankfully the goals which got us to Wembley are etched into my mind. Jimmy Case cracked home the first, at the Clock End of the ground in front of thousands of jubilant Brighton fans. A free-kick about 30 yards out was backheeled to him and he whacked the ball with the outside of his foot and it sailed past Bolder into the top corner. It was a brilliant goal and I remember we all ran after Jimmy and jumped all over him to celebrate!

Wednesday equalised in the second half when a free-kick played into the box from the right-hand side caused mayhem and left two payers through facing goalkeeper Graham Moseley. They couldn't score but the ball broke to substitute Ante Mirocevic, who netted from two yards. That was gutting.

We needn't have worried, though. With about 15 minutes to go Jimmy Case played the ball through for Gordon Smith to run onto and go round the keeper. There were plenty of defenders back however and he cut inside, over-running the ball a bit, but it fell for Michael Robinson to plant a shot into the corner of the net in front of the famous North Bank at Highbury. We were 2-1 ahead and there seemed no way back for the Second Division side now. We held out firmly, with the odd scare, to clinch a trip to the Twin Towers for the first time in the club's history.

The main thing I can remember about the day is how it felt at the final whistle when we had won through to Wembley despite Wednesday's spirited display. I also recall the din the Albion fans made that day. There were 20,000 fans that had made the trip up from Brighton – but at the end it seemed like there were twice that number there because it was all Brighton and Hove Albion. It was a tremendous few minutes on the pitch after the referee blew for time. Utterly memorable.

There was not a lot of live football on television in those days and so the Cup final was much bigger than it is today. It was a real sporting event that the whole country watched – and millions more tuned in around the world. I remember the build up to the semi-finals was that there were two unfashionable sides vying to get to Wembley, Sheffield Wednesday and Brighton and, in the other tie, two very fashionable sides – Arsenal and Manchester United. We had already knocked Liverpool out, along with Manchester City, but we knew having beaten Sheffield Wednesday, whoever we got in the final we would have a glamour club.

We were all a bit sad that we went down that year, but in fact the damage was done in the league long before the semi-final was played and we were very realistic about it, so it made sense to try and grab as much glory as we could in the Cup final. Every game in that run was special for its own reason, but there are not many better feelings than winning a semi-final, and knowing that you are going to Wembley. I won at Wembley with Luton Town in the 1987 League Cup final, beating Arsenal 3-2 in dramatic game – but that feeling, knowing you've made it to the final is pretty special. I think for a lot of people associated with the club that is their best Albion memory. It is a tremendous memory to have, not just the players and the fans, but for the whole town. Everybody knew that we were going to Wembley for the FA Cup final and even though it was a month away it was a most fantastic feeling.

It felt as if we were on a rollercoaster in the weeks before Wembley: singing, doing gigs, making videos and making records. In those days that is what all the clubs who reached cup finals did – there was almost a set pattern to follow – and we all had a good laugh doing it.

Then on 30th April disaster struck for me personally, as I picked up a booking for dissent at Notts County which meant I would be suspended from the final under the totting up procedure. The whole system was so antiquated back then that I was booked at the end of April, but the suspension didn't kick in until three weeks later. The club went to court to try and get it overturned, which was a nice touch. Being the captain, they wanted me to lead the team out on the day. It was also a nice touch to see Tony Grealish, who skippered the side at Wembley, donning a headband in my honour!

Obviously not being involved on the Saturday I was able to relax a bit more than those playing and watched the game unfold from the bench. The 2-2 draw after extra-time meant a replay on the following Thursday – and I was probably the only man connected with Brighton who benefited from Gordon Smith's famous miss. Nobody got cross with Gordon, he was one of the team – and we all appreciated he had played his socks off that day, and given us the lead after 15 minutes.

We tried to treat the replay the same as the final, and I would be lying if I said I didn't get nervous. Everyone gets nerves. If you didn't it would mean you didn't care, and you would not be able to go out on the pitch and perform – but we tried to treat the FA Cup Final as a normal game. Most players are superstitious and everyone does their own thing, but we didn't want to go out of our normal comfort zone. We tried not to treat any game differently from, any other game. Manchester United put four past us in the replay, but I think every player involved in that run had something to be extremely proud of – even if we'd fallen at the final hurdle. It was a huge achievement, arguably the biggest in the club's history. With the way football has gone in recent years, you would question if Brighton will ever play in another FA Cup Final.

Gordon Smith said that he is often asked if he would have given up Wembley to stay in the First Division, and the answer is always no – I agree with that 100%, you would have to pick Wembley. I know that the club has suffered in the subsequent years. Indeed I was back at the club during the final years at the Goldstone and saw it with my own eyes, and that did hurt. But everybody – the players, staff, fans – have always got that day at Wembley to look back on. Brighton and Hove Albion went to Wembley – and not for a play-off final or another trophy – but to take part in the FA Cup Final.

In fact it was twice in six days that we played at the Twin Towers, when that really meant something. Younger readers might not appreciate what the FA Cup meant back then, but even that replay on the Thursday night – yes we lost – but that is something that will never happen again, because now everything has to be done and dusted on the day, with extra-time and penalties. These days, with all that, and the semi-finals being played at Wembley, for me the gloss has been taken off the Cup final.

Any achievements that you have stem from the club that you are playing for and if you play in a successful team then you get recognition – but I probably played the best football of my career when I was at Oxford United, because, to be blunt, we were not very good and I was under pressure in every minute of every game. When I was at Brighton, and then at Luton, most of the time I used to stand at the half-way line and watched the play unfold as we won three or four nil, and I didn't actually have to do much. People then used to say, "what a good player," but when I had to really work hard was when I was playing for Oxford, third from bottom and under pressure week after week.

Of course I returned to Brighton at the end of my career and that was great – but it was spoilt by the turmoil going on at the club at the time. That was caused by non-football people, whose names I won't even sour these pages by mentioning. It's good to see the club come out of that and survive, because there were times when the future looked bleak – and of course the Albion supporters have played a massive part in that.

When I look back at my career, I played a lot of games in the top division; I played for England, and went to a World Cup Finals in 1982, where I played alongside Glenn Hoddle, who was probably the best player I every played with. I played in the League Cup final at Wembley twice. We beat Arsenal one year and then went back the following year and lost to Brian Clough's Nottingham Forest 1-3.

Of course, walking up to the Royal Box and picking up the Littlewoods trophy is something that I will always remember, but getting to Wembley with a bunch of best mates at Brighton was the best experience of my career and that semi-final was certainly the Albion match of my life.

GARY STEVENS
DEFENDER/MIDFIELD 1978–1983

BORN   30 March 1962
DEBUT   15 September 1979
ALBION CAREER   152 games, 3 goals

Perhaps one of the easiest choices for the Albion match of their life was for Gary Stevens. Before moving to Spurs and winning international honours with England, he only ever played for Brighton in the First Division, making 152 appearances between 1979 and 1983, scoring three goals. One of those came in the Albion match of his life: the 1983 FA Cup final.

Brighton & Hove Albion 2 v Manchester United 2 (aet)

FA Cup final
Saturday 21 May 1983

Wembley Stadium
Attendance 100,000

*Stevens nets the vital equaliser as Brighton push United all the way
in a tumultuous FA Cup final*

Teams

Jimmy Melia	Managers	Ron Atkinson
Graham Moseley	1	Gary Bailey
Chris Ramsey	2	Mike Duxbury
(Sub. Gerry Ryan)		
Graham Pearce	3	Arthur Albiston
Tony Grealish	4	Ray Wilkins
Gary Stevens	5	Kevin Moran
Steve Gatting	6	Gordon McQueen
Jimmy Case	7	Bryan Robson
Gary Howlett	8	Arnold Muhren
Michael Robinson	9	Frank Stapleton
Gordon Smith	10	Norman Whiteside
Neil Smillie	11	Alan Davies
Smith 14, Stevens 87	Goals	Stapleton 55, Wilkins 72

Referee: A Grey (Great Yarmouth)

I SIGNED FOR BRIGHTON IN THE summer of 1978 from Ipswich where I had been since the age of 11. At 14 I had signed schoolboy forms with them, but at 16 I was released by the club and told there wasn't really a path forward for me. Bobby Robson [the then-Ipswich boss who would later hand Stevens seven England caps] called me into his office and, to give him his due, as manager of the club he did it – he didn't leave it to the youth team coach. Bobby told me, "Listen, there's not really an opportunity here for you; there are lots of good players ahead of you."

That was true. Ipswich had England pair Russell Osman and Terry Butcher, Scotland international George Burley and others who all played in the same position as me. They had an awful lot of good central defenders to be fair, and Bobby suggested maybe I could get a job locally, and continued to train and play with the youth team on a Saturday morning and that perhaps things would change; or he asked did I want to try my luck elsewhere?

I believed that I could make it and I quickly decided that I wanted to go elsewhere. At the time Ipswich had good connections with Brighton. Added to that my dad used to work with Ken Craggs in semi-professional football years ago, and Ken was working with Alan Mullery at Brighton. Mullery also knew Bobby Robson well, so it seemed the natural move to make. I came down to Brighton with another couple of talented youngsters from Ipswich, including a lad called Joe Peck who didn't make it.

Ipswich were in the top flight at the time and Brighton were one league down in the old Second Division and so it was an opportunity for me to make my mark. I came down to the Goldstone Ground on a two-week trial. The two weeks turned into a month before they made their mind up. Brighton's youth team used to play in the Under-18 Sussex Youth League and my first game was away at Burgess Hill. I scored a goal in that game on the Sunday morning, and John Shepherd and Mick Fogden – the two guys in charge – saw something in me and they pushed for me to be signed on permanently by the club, but it took a month to convince the powers that be.

I remember thinking it was all a bit strange to start with. Brighton was a very different set-up to the one I had become used to at Ipswich, where the training pitch was alongside the stadium in Portman Road. At the Goldstone you had to clip clop up the Old Shoreham Road, over the traffic lights across the road and into Hove Park. The facilities really were poor compared with Ipswich.

Ipswich would crop up a few times at landmarks in my career. I made my debut for Brighton in the latter months of 1979, just over a year after I had joined the club, ironically against Ipswich. Later that season I scored my first goal for the Albion, away to Ipswich, and Bobby Robson was still the manager there at the time. I don't recall him saying anything to me after scoring that goal, but by all accounts I spun round and ran towards the directors' box. I don't remember doing it, but it got in a few local papers that I had stuck two fingers up at the directors' box at Ipswich. If I did do that it was totally disrespectful, but I honestly don't remember actually sticking my fingers up at him. Ipswich Town is a lovely football club and I have an awful lot of respect for them and of course Bobby Robson.

By the time I made my Albion debut in that match at Portman Road, Brighton had won promotion to the First Division for the first and only time in the club's history. I had not played any part in the promotion season, but was lucky enough to be included on the trip up to Newcastle United for the last game, which saw the team clinch promotion. We went up to Tyneside on the Wednesday and I acted as the assistant kit man to Glen Wilson. It was a great experience for me to be involved.

I was 17 when I made my debut the following season. I played on the Saturday morning for the youth team in a friendly away at Queens Park Rangers, and I remember a young Dean Wilkins – who joined Albion shortly after I left – was playing for Rangers. After the game the youth team travelled across London to White Hart Lane to watch Brighton take on Spurs in the First Division. I was stood behind the goal with all the Brighton fans and Mark Lawrenson got injured about 30 yards in front of me. It never crossed my mind at the time, but as a result of Lawro's injury, I would soon be making my debut for the first team. Lawro was out for a while and Mullers called me in early the following week to tell me that I was in the first team on Saturday, for the match at home to Ipswich – and I had four or five days to panic about it!

It was a week of anticipation and huge build up for me, but credit to Alan Mullery, who had seen me play for the youth team and also regularly for the reserves. In those days we didn't have a huge squad and I was the reserve team centre-half in the mould of Mark Lawrenson to an extent, and so he stuck me in.

Over the five years I was with the Albion, we had the promotion and four years in the top flight. Those years must rank up as the very best for the club, but the cup run in my final year at the club trumped even that. There was a bizarre sort of momentum that went with it and each time the draw for the next round came along we were all saying who we would like to be paired with and invariably we were getting one or other of the teams that we wanted in every draw. Even when we drew Liverpool in the fifth round they were the team we wanted as it was a massive glamour tie and a big money-spinner for the club to go to Anfield at that stage in the competition. To then go and win was unbelievable!

When you look at the semi-final draw we could have come out of the hat with Manchester United or Arsenal, but instead we got Sheffield Wednesday, who were then in the Second Division. Everything went our way and you do need that good fortune to be successful to a certain extent, but we also had a lot of good players. We had internationals in the squad and other players who would later go on to play international football. We were a highly talented side without doubt. I have always said that a good run in the cup helps your league form and I strongly believe that – although our example doesn't back that up. I personally think that we had enough quality and enough good players in the side to avoid relegation.

In 1983 the FA Cup final was a much bigger event than it perhaps is today. In that era it was one of the few live 90 minutes of football shown on TV each season. It was the showpiece game of the year for football. A crowd of 100,000 at Wembley on the Saturday, plus I don't know how many millions watching it on the television in England, but the truth of the matter is that there were hundreds of millions watching the match world-wide.

Thankfully I played a game which I felt ranked as one of my best-ever performances. Sometimes in my role as a pundit I have been critical of the opinions and the thoughts of the punters who vote for man-of-the-match, but on this occasion it was the BBC viewers who selected me for that accolade over the two matches. If you are going to have a great game it is brilliant to do it in a high profile match and that is exactly what happened to me. It was just a shame we couldn't cause an upset and get a win either on the Saturday or the Thursday evening.

I remember the week or ten days leading up to the final were just busy, busy, busy. The local TV wanted you to do pretty much everything, so there is footage of me sat on the funfair rides on the seafront; the local radio wanted you; the national papers came down and wanted photographs. There were individual interviews to do and the clamour for tickets was unbelievable. I had friends and relations crawling out of the woodwork wanting tickets and, of course, they all assumed that as a player I could get them one.

It was a actually a relief when we finally got on the coach to go up to the Selsdon Park Hotel near Croydon on the Friday, and then on the Saturday morning the excitement of the helicopter flight across London was a healthy distraction for everybody. The club was sponsored by British Caledonian that season and they had laid on one of their helicopters to fly us all to Wembley in style. My recollection of flying across the city was just how much green area there was in the capital. The weather wasn't particularly great and of course we had those ridiculous white jackets and shoes on. I remember Jimmy Case refused to wear it. He went in his own suit and hung it on the fact that he always bought a suit for a cup final and that was his superstition!

I remember landing at a local school nearby to the stadium and then there was the coach ride up Wembley Way, surrounded by all the supporters milling around. It felt slightly strange. What we were doing was something that I had watched religiously every year on the television since the age of five – the build up to the Cup final and then the Cup final itself – but rather than watching it I was actually part of it.

It was quite a long way into the game before I even had my first touch of the ball. I intercepted a pass and went through a tackle, keeping possession. At that point I had a feeling it was going to turn out to be a good day for me. I recall we had a few scares early on. United went close with an Alan Davies header fairly early, but then against the odds Gordon Smith put us in front with an excellent header from Gary Howlett's brilliant cross. After that we thought that maybe it was going to be our day.

The atmosphere; the fans and the banners stand out in my mind when I think back – although there seemed to be more red and white than blue and white in the stadium. I remember that the Norman Whiteside tackle on Chris Ramsey infuriated me. It was a bad tackle and perhaps cost us the game. We were 1-0 up at the time and they scored through Whiteside shortly after Chris got injured, but while he was still on the pitch, struggling with the injury. In those days we only had one substitute and Gerry Ryan came on and did a great job at right-back, even though he was a midfield player; but we did miss Chris because he had been having a great game.

Ray Wilkins put United ahead fairly early in the second half, and that was a cracking goal. Ray cut in from the right hand side and curled the ball into the far top corner with his left foot. Pure class, but perhaps now it seemed it wasn't to be for us.

I remember it was late in the game and we were 2-1 behind, which was a bit harsh on us, when we won a corner. I hadn't scored a goal all season for the club and I wasn't even going up for corners at that point. I can remember looking across to the dugout where Jimmy Melia and suspended skipper Steve Foster were waving me to get up the park. I went forward and Jimmy Case knocked the ball to the edge of the area from the corner. I'm not sure if Tony Grealish was trying to pick out a pass or whether it was a shot, but I don't think he struck the ball as well as he would have liked. I was running in with a view to hitting a shot and it fell perfectly at my feet. I took one touch to control it then I drove it as hard as I could towards the target. I struck the ball really cleanly and it did exactly what I intended – beat United's Gary Bailey and hit the back of the net!

Then it was a case of comparing my celebration with that of Ray Wilkins. Ray set off and almost did a lap of honour while I just shook hands with a couple of the boys. I wasn't a goal scorer and I didn't have a goal celebration; I didn't know how to celebrate a goal because it was not something that I did on a regular basis!

We probably deserved to win the match after that, and Gordon Smith had that famous chance in the last minute of extra-time – but at the time I certainly didn't see it as a bad miss by Gordon, I thought that Gary Bailey made a great save. I think that the truth is that having got to the FA Cup final against Manchester United and to have taken them to extra-time and got a replay out of it, before the game we would have settled for that without doubt. I don't think that there was any feeling of having blown our chance or anything like that in the camp. The general feeling was that it was good news that we had another go at it and another trip to Wembley. I don't know how Gordon felt at the time, whether he felt that it was a great opportunity that he had missed or not, but I certainly didn't see it that way.

We took the helicopter back to Brighton and we virtually followed the flow of the A23 all the way back so we could see the fans returning in convoys. We landed on the sports grounds at the Brighton & Hove Sixth Form College and travelled down to the Brighton Centre for the reception. A mate of mine bought me a jeroboam of champagne and that was waiting for me there. I'm not sure if it got drunk on the night or if I took it home and drank it there, but for a number of years I had the empty bottle as a memento.

The BBC telephoned on the Sunday to ask if I would go on Breakfast Time on the Monday morning, but I refused to do it on the basis that we had the game coming up a few days later and it wasn't the ideal way of preparing. I stepped clear of all the furore that was continuing on and tried to stay focused and do the training.

I think that in the replay for the first 25 minutes or so we probably played better than we did on the Saturday. Over two games against Manchester United, though, the chances were that we were not going to win, and ultimately it became like a two-legged final. The odds were stacked against us and maybe in hindsight our greatest chance had been in the first game. We didn't take that chance, though, and therefore the odds were even further against us in the replay.

To lose by four goals was very disappointing. Bryan Robson had an inspired evening and scored twice, while Norman Whiteside continued his incredible rise to stardom by also netting before half-time. The game was all but over then and Arnold Muhren's penalty rounded off the scoring half way through the second half.

The replay proved my final game for Brighton – although I had absolutely no intention of leaving and didn't believe for a minute that I would be. I was, after all, in the throes of trying to buy another house. I was living in Mile Oak at the time and was thinking of buying a house in Hove Park. I remember the people I was buying off asked me why I was buying their house when I was moving! I told that I wasn't going anywhere, but then out of the blue I then got a call from Jimmy Melia while I was visiting my parents. He told me that the club had agreed to sell me to Tottenham and asked did I want to go? My immediate reaction was to ask him why they were selling me? Didn't they want to get promotion back to the First Division? I guess for Brighton the money being offered was a big thing, especially after the club had dropped out of the First Division. They got £300,000 for me – which was a decent fee at the time – and I went and had a chat with Tottenham. Bill Nicholson, their legendary double-winning manager who was still involved in the club, took me to see their training ground and sold the club to me.

It wasn't a difficult decision to go to a big club from a side that had just got relegated, but I would have happily stayed at Brighton. You might think that a very naïve response. Fortunately for me the move to Spurs proved a fabulous one and I had seven great years at White Hart Lane. I played in another FA Cup final and won the UEFA Cup. I got into the England Under 21s on a regular basis and established myself as an England squad player under Bobby Robson and went to the World Cup Finals in Mexico in 1986. No disrespect, but that wouldn't have happened had I stayed at Brighton. Of course it came up – and Bobby knew it would come up – that the kid he rejected as a 16-year-old schoolboy was going to play for England, but times had moved on and the decision Bobby had made at the time was right for him and for Ipswich. It benefited the Albion and it benefited me – because without it I wouldn't have had five fantastic years with the club which culminated in those unforgettable Cup final appearances.

BARRY LLOYD
MANAGER 1987–1993

BORN   19 February 1949
FIRST GAME   10 January 1987
ALBION CAREER   371 games

Barry Lloyd spent six years at the Albion as manager between 1987 and 1993 – but his time in charge was beset by financial and off-field problems – a legacy of the club's First Division days. Hindsight shows him to have done a fine job in often difficult circumstances. In his first full season, 1987/88, the club won promotion from Division Three, against the odds, and he very nearly led the club to a top-flight return in 1991, via the play-offs on a shoestring budget. The 6-2 win against Millwall, over two legs in the play-off semi-final, which set up a Wembley final with Notts County is Barry's Match of his Albion Life.

Brighton & Hove Albion 4 v Millwall 1

League Division Two Play-off semi-final first leg
Sunday 19 May 1991

Goldstone Ground
Attendance 15,390

*Brighton tear Millwall apart to come from behind and rack up a big lead
in the battle for a Wembley final spot*

Teams

Barry Lloyd	Managers	Bruce Rioch
Perry Digweed	1	Brian Horne
Gary Chivers	2	Keith Stevens
Steve Gatting	3	Ian Dawes
Dean Wilkins	4	Gary Waddock
		(Sub. Les Briley)
		(Sub. Mick McCarthy)
Colin Pates	5	David Thompson
Nicky Bissett	6	Alan McLeary
Mark Barham	7	Paul Stephenson
Stefan Iovan	8	Jon Goodman
Mike Small	9	Teddy Sheringham
Robert Codner	10	Alex Rae
Clive Walker	11	Paul Kerr
(Sub. John Robinson)		
Barham 40, Small 53, Walker 55, Codner 59	Goals	Stephenson 14

Referee: K Hackett (Sheffield)

My INTEREST IN FOOTBALL WAS born from watching my father play reserve team football for Hayes in the Athenian League as a young boy. He never did get beyond the reserves, but he passed on his love of the game to me during my formative years and I think he was proud of what I achieved in the game both as a player and a manager. Dad loved the game. He passed away in July 2008 at the age 84, but he was still going to watch football.

I joined Chelsea as a schoolboy. I was fortunate to play for London and West London as a youth and I had a choice of any number of clubs to join, but I chose Chelsea because of the West London connection. In 1969 I was sold to Fulham for £30,000. That was a fair old fee in those days and in today's market it would be more like £3 million! I had some great times at Fulham with the players they had there – the likes of George Best, Bobby Moore and Alan Mullery. I spent a terrific eleven years of my life at Fulham and I loved every minute of my time there. In 1975 we reached the FA Cup Final, but I didn't play. Then I had a huge cultural change as I headed to the Westcountry to join Yeovil – who were not in the Football League back then, but were renowned as cup giant killers; and it was a step on the managerial ladder for me.

After three years at Yeovil I landed the job at Worthing. I got that job thanks to Alan Mullery, my old Fulham team-mate. The job was vacant, and I was back in West London after leaving Yeovil and it was Alan who told me to take the job. I came down to the south coast and in two successive seasons we were good enough on the field to win promotion to today's equivalent of the Blue Square Premier – in those days it was called the Gola League – but our Woodside Road ground wasn't up to scratch so we weren't allowed to progress. Financially it would also have been difficult for Worthing to compete at the higher level, so perhaps it was for the best.

I eventually left Worthing when I was offered the chance to move back into full-time football as assistant and reserve team manager at the Albion. Alan Mullery had arguably been the club's most successful manager during his first spell in charge at the club in the 1970s and he was brought back to Brighton after the board decided to part company with previous manager Chris Cattlin. Alan invited me to join his coaching staff. As things turned out he didn't stay very long in the job, but that's often the way things work out in football. I have never been one to pay too much attention to what is written in newspapers, I think managers need to be their own men, and I wasn't reading many papers at the time of Alan's departure, but I have since learned that the media speculation as to why he left the job was that he had a lack of commitment. As someone who was working closely with him at the time, I do not believe he didn't have total commitment to the cause – but for a number of reasons it was very much tougher for him second time around.

I was given the opportunity to succeed Alan in January 1987, but the club was in a terrible state after overspending on long contracts during its four-year spell in the First Division. It was a traumatic time in the club's history and we went 15 games without a win. I thought to myself 'Do I really need all this?' The fans were on my back all the time, yet I never I knew from one game to the next what the team would be for the next game. The squad Mullers had inherited needed investment, and he wasn't able to do that because of boardroom constraints. Needless to say I wasn't allowed to do that either; in fact my brief when I was given the job was very clear: cut the wage bill. Everybody was put up for sale. I even remember The *Evening Argus* running a front page story that advertised every full-time professional at the club as available to buy. That turmoil surrounding the club made it difficult and against that backdrop it was inevitable the club would be relegated that season.

I was forced to sell the club's better players; it was a simple choice between keeping the players and going out of business or surviving. I think between taking over the job from Alan, and the start of the following season, I cleared out 18 players in total – including popular men such as Terry Connor, Dean Saunders and Danny Wilson. I had little choice in the sale of any of the players, but once we'd cleared the decks I was given a little bit of money to invest during the close season. Despite a new-look squad the fans began the 1987/88 season low on confidence, but I had every confidence in the squad of players I had assembled. I knew we would do well and as it turned out we won promotion on the final day of the season with a 2-1 win at the Goldstone Ground over Bristol Rovers.

We had a completely new-look side: Doug Rougvie and Keith Dublin formed the backbone of the defence, with John Keeley, plucked from non-league Chelmsford, in commanding form behind them between the sticks. In midfield we had Alan Curbishley and Dean Wilkins – back at the club after a spell playing in the Dutch First Division – and up front Kevin Bremner proved the perfect foil to Garry Nelson, who for much of the season looked as if he was going to break Peter Ward's goals-in-a-season record. Garry had played much of his career as a midfielder, but I had signed him specifically to partner Kevin, a typical robust centre-forward, up front. The pairing proved excellent for us that season, and it was fitting that they scored the two goals which won us promotion on the final day.

The following season, 1988/89, playing in what is now the Championship, we comfortably stayed up and I felt that was a terrific campaign.

Once again we had to bolster the team after about a dozen games, but we fought hard to establish ourselves and played some good football to stay in the division which again was a great achievement given the financial problems that continued to engulf the club. We consolidated in 1989/90 and ended the season with Ukranian Sergei Gotsmanov in the side. He ended up joining Southampton, then in the First Division, ahead of the 1990/91 season. We had invested a little bit of the money we had received for Keith Dublin and John Keeley, whose sales to Watford and Oldham had yielded around half a million pounds. Mike Small had joined from Greek side PAOK Salonika, while in the September skilful striker John Byrne arrived from French club Le Havre, where he'd fallen out of favour. We hadn't made a great start to the season, so John's arrival gave us some impetus and got our season going.

The club's financial predicament had forced me to begin recruiting players from the continent. As well as Mike Small, I had plucked Dean Wilkins from PEC Zwolle and I got chatting to a number of agents during that period and realised there were quite a few English players playing in Europe. I didn't go looking for foreign-based players initially – but I learned of the number of English players playing abroad, virtually unnoticed, and John and Mike were two of those. I'd tried to sign John 18 months earlier when he was at QPR, so I was surprised, given his qualities, how little interest was shown by other clubs in England given how well he'd done at York under manager Denis Smith and then QPR. John moved to Le Havre for £200,000 and at the time there was no way we could match that fee, but I kept an interest in what John was doing over there and then lo and behold at the start of 1990/91 season I had an agent call me to say he was available. The original fee the club was quoted was a farcical amount of

Heroes from yesteryear: left, 1958 Hove-born hero: five-star
Adrian Thorne; center, dependable defender Norman Gall;
and, right, 1972 promotion-winner Ken Beamish.

Whizz on the run. Goldstone idol Peter Ward on the attack, watched by
Paul Clark and Brian Horton.

Left, Albion's greatest skipper of all time? There is no doubt Brian Horton was the on-field driving force behind the club's rise to the top flight in the late 1970s. Centre, a goalscoring full-back. Gary Williams signed from Preston and played a major role in helping Albion to the First Division and staying there! Right, another Albion captain fantastic, central defender Steve Foster. Fozzie filled the void left by Brian Horton and led the Seagulls all the way to Wembley

Left, Jimmy Case celebrates netting the opening goal of the 1983 FA Cup semi-final, while, right, Steve Foster's best pal Michael Robinson scores the winning goal to take Brighton to Wembley.

Gary Stevens score the goal against Manchester United which levelled the scores at 2-2 in the 1983 FA Cup final at Wembley.

Down, beaten, but not disgraced. He might not have known it on the night, but Cup Final man-of-the-match Gary Stevens waves farewell to the Albion supporters.

Success on a shoestring ... Barry Lloyd took Albion to Wembley and within 90 minutes of a return to the First Divsion - but sadly Notts County won the 1991 play-off final, with Tommy Johnson, right, setting them on their way with the opening goal.

The MOST important goal in Albion's history. Robbie Reinelt levels at Hereford, a goal which saves the club from relegation out of the Football League (at Hereford's expense) ... and almost certain extinction.

Robbie Reinelt celebrates securing Brighton's
league status at Edgar Street in 1997.

All smiles. Danny Cullip, left, and Michel Kuipers celebrate after
Cullip's goal gave the Albion victory over Chesterfield and the
first of back-to-back championships.

Bobby Zamora celebrates one of his goals in ten successive games which helped Albion to the League One title in 2002.

Zamora shakes hands with supporters after the final game of the 2001/02 season has seen Albion clinch the championship and promotion back to the second tier of English football.

Leon Knight scores the penalty which beats Bristol City in the
2004 Play-off final to secure a quick return back to the Championship.

Back at the first attempt. Charlie and co celebrate at the Millennium after
a playoff final win over Bristol City means promotion back to the second
tier of English football.

Guy Butters was a lynchpin during Brighton's bid for Championship survival in the 2004/05 season, clinched with a tense draw against Ipswich. Here he celebrates his vital goal in a 1-0 win at West Ham.

Manager Russell Slade acknowledges supporters, left, and, right, is chaired off the pitch by exultant fans after Albion's dramatic win over Stockport spares them from relegation in May 2009.

money and totally out of our league, but as time went by we managed to convince Le Havre that John should make the move just over the Channel – that was why it took so long to complete the deal.

Our results until December were fairly average, but we stayed in touch with the play-off picture and then we really clicked when the FA Cup came around. We beat Scunthorpe in the third round and that set up a fourth round tie at Liverpool. We went to Anfield at the end of January and got a 2-2 draw, fighting back from two goals down, and from that moment on the side played a different brand of football. We should have won the replay at the Goldstone, where we were far and away the better side on the night. They only nicked it in the last minute of extra time with Ian Rush toe-ending one in and Steve McMahon netting the other. However the way we played gave us such a lot of confidence – and with the media predicting a cup hangover in the league we won our next league game away at Charlton, completing the double over the South Londoners in the process. After that we were never out of the top six and at one point we looked like we might even push into the automatic places. But we had a disastrous run after Easter, and it was disappointing that we didn't sail into the play-offs. We should have clinched our place with three or four games to go, but left it not only to the last game against Ipswich but to the last minute too when Dean Wilkins scored his famous last-gasp free-kick. I remember sitting on the bench and praying for Dean just to hit the target in the great style I knew he was capable.

That set up a two-legged play-off semi-final with Millwall. The first leg was played on a Sunday lunchtime at the Goldstone, and we knew it was going to be a tense affair over the two games. Having finished sixth in the table, we were the underdogs and at home in the first leg which gave them the advantage of playing at home in the second leg. Millwall also had the psychological advantage, having beaten us 3-0 only a few weeks earlier in the league. They had a good side containing the likes of Alan McLeary, Phil Babb, Keith Stevens and Teddy Sheringham.

Ahead of the match, I knew how we approached the game was impor-tant. We couldn't afford to be faint hearted and I wanted the players to just go out there and have a go. That was our philosophy right the way through the first leg and we went at them from the first minute. I think we surprised them a little bit because I think they thought we'd be defensive, but we hit the ground running. Even after Paul Stephenson put Millwall ahead, there was a great response from the players and an equaliser from Mark Barham.

That was alucky goal in some ways. Perry Digweed put in one of his incredibly long punts and the ball was about to bounce on the edge of the Millwall box when centre-half Thompson ducked under it, I think intending to allow it to bounce through to Brian Horne in the visitors' goal. But as he took his eye off the ball he also turned his back and the ball actually landed on the back of his head and squirted off right into Mark's path. The little winger raced in and cracked the ball into the bottom corner. It really was a vital goal so close to the interval and the fans knew it. A load of them raced onto the pitch in celebration. Sometimes things just go for you.

A manager's job is in preparing his side for a game, there is very little you can do during a game. You can change tactics and personnel, but in those days your options on the bench were limited to two subs – but the one opportunity you have as a manager is the half-time team talk. Mark Barham had struck an equaliser before break, which gave us the perfect boost for the second half. I can't remember what I said at half-time – I've given so many team talks in my managerial career – but whatever it was it worked! It would have been along the lines of push on and keep playing the way you have been and I am sure the goals will come . . . and they did, as after the break Mike Small, Clive Walker and Robert Codner capped some excellent football with a display of clinical finishing.

Mike's goal also owed something to the Millwall defence as the ball ended up being played into his path by a bad piece of control by one of the back four on the edge of the box. Mike lashed the ball in to give us a 2-1 lead and suddenly it was all Brighton.

Small flicked on a long ball and evergreen winger Clive Walker raced clear to plant his shot into the net. Then the fourth goal in particular was really well worked. Millwall were pressing looking for a consolation goal to give them something to hold onto to take back to the Den, but we broke and the ball was played up to Small in the centre circle. He played a lovely touch to Robert Codnor who was haring in towards goal and he took the ball on and easily beat Horne with his right foot with a cool finish. The place went barmy then. It was absolutely packed that day and fans spilled onto the pitch again, while all around there was a sea of happy faces and blue and white scarves.

Small was such a handful that day. Millwall couldn't really cope with him. He had had a great season for us, scoring 21 goals in all, and Mike was a massive part of our success and why we reached the play-off final.

Going into the second leg 4-1 ahead, many of our fans were already gripped by Wembley fever, but I knew we still had a lot of work to do to ensure we got to the final. Millwall, with their 3-0 league win still fresh in the memory, went in front early in the game and with a fanatical and partisan home crowd urging them on the second leg was a very, very tense affair. It always was difficult to play in the intimidating atmosphere of the old Den at Cold Blow Lane. There had been a lot of tension in the dressing room before the game. Having won 4-1 I could sense the players were thinking 'crikey we can't afford to make mistakes and blow this,' and it was my job to ensure that they relaxed for the game.

After conceding that early goal, and suffering a couple of other early scares, once again my players were brave. We had Garry Nelson playing a very high line in attack – we didn't want him coming back and helping out in defence; we wanted him stretching their defence and that worked very well for us as eventually we got the breakthrough as Robert Codnor scored to make it 5-2 on aggregate. That effectively killed off the tie. Robert was much criticised during his time with Albion, but if you look at the statistics and look at the games on videos, in particular during that season, he was excellent for us. He was involved in around 50 to 60 per cent of the season's goals and he thrived alongside the quality players we had brought in for that season.

The play-off final itself was a huge disappointment. Not because the players didn't perform – they did – but because we just didn't get the rub of the green on the day. I left out Garry Nelson because John Byrne was fit again and for no other reason. Garry made a lot about where and how I broke the news to him that he wasn't playing, but I think that was irrelevant. There is no easy way to tell any player he isn't playing in a game, let alone a Wembley final. If you look back at the stats and the amount of games he played that season, I think wherever he was told didn't really matter. Yes it was a sad way for Garry to bow out, and he'd been excellent for us in the semi-final, but he had only played in the game at Millwall because of an injury to John Byrne. John – who had been a huge player for us that season – was fit for the final and it was the right decision that Garry should make way for him. To me there was no story, but there would have been a huge outcry if I'd left John or Mike Small out of the squad. John, who got injured winning the free-kick which Dean had fired in against Ipswich, had needed a cartilage operation, and I had the same injury at the same time myself and John actually took my place in the queue for the operating table! I did mine on the training ground a week earlier and was booked in for an operation, but after he did his against Ipswich, I let him take my place. To have John fit for a potential play-off final was much more important than me than my own discomfort!

Of course no Albion fan needs reminding that we lost the Wembley game 3-1. We simply didn't get the breaks on the day: we hit the woodwork twice and their first goal came from a very dubious corner – but the team gave it their all and that is all I could ask.

I've heard it said that we couldn't afford to win promotion – but it was the complete opposite. To keep that team together – and ultimately add to it – we couldn't afford not to get promotion. That summer Mike Small, who had done so well all season, was sold to West Ham and again I was obliged to sell most of the squad. Without our star players it was inevitable that things would not be as good the following season. That summer I was also offered jobs with Chelsea and Southampton, both in the First Division, but felt I had unfinished business with Brighton. Instead Chelsea appointed Ian Porterfield and Saints Ian Branfoot. With hindsight, perhaps I should have taken the opportunity to manage at the top level, but I like to think I helped the club survive one of its most rocky periods. I moved into a managing director role and we were constantly staving off winding up orders and appearing in the high court.

Despite all that, the supporters, having seen the club go so close in the previous campaign, expected us to have another push for promotion – but with budgets again being cut that just wasn't possible. Brighton Independent Supporters Association appeared – and there was a lot of anger at the way things were being run – but I think some fans appreciated the precarious financial state of the club. I could accept I wasn't popular the way things were going on the pitch, but I was also trying to keep the club stable in role as MD. Subsequently there has been enough written about Greg Stanley and Bill Archer and what they did to the club, but it was ironic that David Bellotti became the most popular man at the club by sacking me! After their takeover went through, it was obvious they cared little about the club, and I knew they were going to sell the ground. If I hadn't cared so much I would have walked out, but I was trying to save the club.

I think if we'd won the play-off final I could have kept the club in the top flight for one year until the Sky money came along and who knows what might have happened to the club then. Of course it didn't work out like that and the rest is history. Nonetheless I did a lot of work on plans for a new stadium at Shoreham, but that was abandoned when Archer took over. He had other ideas for the club. I went back to Worthing, although I was not as successful as I had been before, and after a number of coaching and scouting roles it was really pleasing to be offered the job of chief scout back at Brighton. I am enjoying it – I get to watch football, travel and help a club that I love. I also like to think there's a sense of justice that I am back with the Albion now Archer, Stanley and Bellotti are long gone.

ROBBIE REINELT
MIDFIELDER/FORWARD 1997–1998

BORN   11 March 1974
DEBUT   15 February 1997
ALBION CAREER   49 games, 9 goals

While fans may argue as to the best goal scored by a player in a Brighton shirt, there is almost universal unanimity that Robbie Reinelt scored the most important goal in the club's history on 3rd May 1997. Signed from Colchester for £15,000 by manager Steve Gritt, Robbie started fewer than 50 matches for the Seagulls, yet without his equaliser at Hereford on that historic day the very existence of the club would have been in doubt. So for Robbie it was an easy choice for the match of his Albion life.

Hereford United 1 v Brighton & Hove Albion 1

FA Cup Final
Saturday 3 May 1997

Edgar Street
Attendance 8,532

Reinelt's left-footed equaliser saves Brighton's league status
and sparks incredible celebrations

Teams

Graham Turner	Managers	Steve Gritt
Andy de Bont	1	Mark Ormerod
David Norton	2	John Humphrey
Rob Warner	3	Stuart Tuck
John Brough	4	Jeff Minton
Bradley Sandeman	5	Ross Johnson
Trevor Matthewson	6	Mark Morris
Chris Hargreaves	7	Stuart Storer
		(Sub. Gary Hobson)
Brian McGorry	8	Kerry Mayo
Adrian Foster	9	Ian Baird
John Williams	10	Craig Maskell
Tony Agana	11	Paul McDonald
		(Sub. Robbie Reinelt)
Mayo og 21	Goal	Reinelt 63

Referee: N Barry (Scunthorpe)

I STARTED MY FOOTBALL LEAGUE career at Aldershot, for whom I signed as a trainee when I was still a teenager. They were struggling near the bottom of the league during the time I was there and it was a sad day when they went out of business in 1992. I was really delighted to see them get back in the Football league last season.

Throughout my professional career I seemed to make a habit of signing for clubs in crisis. After leaving Aldershot I had a trial for Colchester, which came to nothing and I then joined Wivenhoe, who were in the Isthmian or Ryman League as it's now known. Off the back of that I was able to get back into league football with Gillingham, who signed me a year after Aldershot folded.

Like the Shots, the Gills too were in trouble at the bottom of the Football League and only stayed up by beating Halifax in the last home match of my first season there – but I couldn't be held responsible as I didn't feature until the following season and funnily enough, my debut for the Gills was against Brighton in a League Cup game at the Priestfield Stadium. The ties were played over two legs in those days and I do remember that I scored the only goal in the first leg, but I also remember that Brighton beat us 2-0 at the Goldstone to set up a two-legged second round tie with league champions Manchester United.

I wasn't a prolific goal scorer, but managed to score eight times for the Gills in about sixty odd games. I stayed with Gillingham until March 1995 when I joined Colchester, as part of a deal that saw Steve Brown move in the other direction. I felt I was doing fairly well during my time at Layer Road and was getting good reviews in the media and the fans seemed to take to me, but I picked up an injury and it all went downhill with Colchester manager Steve Wignall after I returned to fitness. We had a couple of disagreements, and I could see that I had no real future at Layer Road, so when Steve Gritt came in for me I jumped at the chance to prove myself at Brighton – even though they were struggling on and off the pitch. At the time the club were bottom of the league, and there was the added uncertainty with the off-field situation and the impending sale of the Goldstone Ground.

A lot of people said I was mad to join Brighton at that time, given that they were bottom of the league, and looked absolute certainties for relegation to the Conference. When I joined the club they were well adrift at the foot of the table, and everyone – even their own fans – was saying that they would go down, but Steve Gritt impressed me from the start. He was confident we could avoid the drop and he was convinced everything would work out in the end. At the time only one club was relegated from the Football League and Steve had this philosophy that he had been brought in to take us off the bottom of the table by the end of the season, and if that meant reaching that target on the final day then that would be mission accomplished.

I had my own reasons for signing as well as I felt I was going stale at Colchester and needed a new challenge and I just thought that Brighton would be good for me.

While I was sure that Steve Gritt was a manager I would enjoy working with, the same cannot be said of David Bellotti, the Chief Executive of the club at the time I joined. I knew he wasn't liked by Brighton supporters, who held him responsible for the club's off-field problems and on-field demise, and I just didn't take to him from the start. What put me off straight away was his greeting of me in the club's offices. To be quite honest, it was like shaking hands with a wet fish, and he could not boast to having what I would call a man's handshake at all.

I never could understand why they had sold the Goldstone Ground. It had obviously destabilised the club and was affecting things on the field.

Just as I knew Bellotti was a figure of hate, I also knew the fans were angry about the situation surrounding the sale. I was also aware how big a club Brighton was, the potential they had and what a large fan base they had. After all, it wasn't that long since they had been in the old First Division and reached the Cup final and I'd heard that just a couple of weeks before I joined the club, over 8,000 fans had flocked to see them beat Hartlepool. I know supporters from around the country came to see them that day to support the Fans United backing for the people who were trying to keep the club alive, but it was still an amazing turnout considering their league position at the time.

My debut came at Carlisle, but it didn't last long. I took a knock after about 20 minutes and had to go off with concussion. I was seeing four players instead of one and there was no way I could continue. We lost that match 2-1 and I was on the substitute's bench for the next game against

Swansea at the Goldstone. I remember it being an exciting match, which we eventually won 3-2, although it wasn't enough to change our league position and we still remained rooted to the bottom of the table.

I returned to the side for the trip to Darlington the following Saturday, but again the away jinx continued as we lost 2-0 – Brighton had won just once away from home that season, and that record remained unchanged, although we did pick up some vital draws on the road. I don't think we played that badly away from home, but the results just didn't go for us and we never seemed to get the rub of the green. It was a completely different story at the Goldstone Ground however, where we were really gaining momentum and starting to make the place a real fortress and my first goal for the club arrived in a midweek game at home to Northampton, which resulted in yet another home victory. Now we were getting up some momentum and consistency and the escape looked possible.

The next Saturday we were at home again, with Leyton Orient as the visitors and we once again played some terrific football and were two goals up in no time. I don't know what happened to us in the second half, but within 15 minutes we suddenly found ourselves behind, and for the first time in some time we found ourselves in danger of losing an excellent unbeaten home record. Orient were well on top, but we managed to get our game together and Ian Baird equalised, only for Orient to go straight up the other end and regain the lead.

At this time feelings were already running high and it was the final straw for a couple of fans, who reacted badly to Orient's fourth goal. I didn't see the initial pitch invasion; all I remember is that they suddenly appeared in front of the Orient players and were having a go at them. I'm not sure what good they hoped to do by running on the pitch – the club had already been deducted points for a pitch invasion – but I remember that Ray Wilkins behaved like an absolute gentleman. Instead of doing what most of us would have done and lash out at them, he tried to reason with them, saying he understood how frustrated they were, while at the same time urging them to get back in the stand. Fortunately calm was quickly restored and the fans removed from the pitch to allow the game to continue. And five minutes from the end we were given a chance to get something out of the game when we were awarded a penalty and our Scottish winger Paul McDonald showed tremendous bottle to step up to take the kick. Paul kept his nerve to score an equaliser and maintain our Goldstone unbeaten record, which stretched back as far as Steve Gritt's appointment.

Despite dropping two points, none of us were despondent about our situation. Steve Gritt continued to take it one game at a time. I know it's an old cliché in football, but that's exactly what he did with us, instilling it into us. We never spoke about the league position at training or in the build up to matches; Steve did things very simply and just focussed our minds on the next league game.

We lost badly at Hull City, going down 3-0 at the old Boothferry Park (it's amazing to think both Brighton and Hull were both struggling right at the bottom of the league just over a decade ago) and I missed the next game – another vital home win over Cardiff City, and with the team over the blip in Yorkshire, I had to settle for a substitute's role in the next three matches. We lost narrowly, 2-1 at Chester, despite leading at the break; beat Barnet in the last-ever floodlit game at the soon-to-be-closed Goldstone; and then lost narrowly again at Scunthorpe, the ironically-named Chris Hope getting the only goal of the game.

It was getting nervy and several fans were beginning to fear the worst after that defeat at Scunthorpe, particularly with champions-elect Wigan due next at the Goldstone Ground. We had four games left to play, and were still adrift at the foot of the table . . . five points adrift of Hereford at this point, but we remained unbeaten in our next four games. I was back in the side for the Wigan game, which we won, thanks to another goal from Craig Maskell. Craig was an excellent player and his experience was vital to us; he came in for a bit of unfair stick at times and certainly didn't get the credit he deserved, and his goals playing a major part in keeping us up. He struck up a great striking partnership with Ian Baird and those two were very important players for the Albion that season.

We picked up a rare point on the road at Cambridge United, and I was fortunate enough to get on the scoresheet with my second goal for the club. Paul Wanless scored early in the game for Cambridge, who were chasing promotion, but we hit back before half-time and that 1-1 draw was a huge, huge result for us. We were still bottom of the table, but knowing we faced Hereford in the final match it meant that our fate was in our own hands. Going into those final two games we all knew that whatever happened elsewhere, if we could win against Doncaster in that emotional final fixture at the Goldstone and then go to Hereford and win then that would be enough to complete the great escape and secure our Football League status.

The final game at the Goldstone Ground against Doncaster was always going to be an emotional affair, particularly for players like Stuart Tuck,

Kerry Mayo and Ross Johnson. They were all local lads and had watched the team from the terraces as youngsters and then graduated through the club's schoolboy and youth teams. It was a huge part of their heritage that was going to be bulldozed within a few weeks. Despite my goal at Cambridge a week earlier, I didn't make the starting eleven for the game, so I was able to watch events unfold from the bench, although naturally I would have preferred to have been playing. Predictably it was tense – there was too much at stake for us for it not be a tense affair. I remember Ian Baird, who was a major player for us, and Doncaster centre-half Darren Moore got involved in a tussle that saw both of them sent off really early in the game. It was a long ball forward which Bairdy was chasing, and the two got tangled up, and the next thing I remember they were trading punches. Darren has gone onto prove himself at the top level, and those who have seen him play know he's a huge guy, but equally Bairdy was a feisty Scotsman, who could handle himself, so it was quite a tussle. Certainly I wouldn't fancy breaking those two up!

In the second half the lads kept going at Doncaster, desperate for a goal to break the deadlock. In the end we won a corner on the right, which Jeff Minton took. The ball bounced about in the Rovers six-yard box for ages, hitting the bar on one occasion from Mark Morris's header, before dropping to Stuart Storer about eight yards out, who had enough time to hammer the ball into the goal to settle an incredibly tense game. It was no more than we deserved and obviously massively important, but a lot of people don't realise how important a part Craig Maskell played in it. As the ball was bobbing around the Rovers box he was on the blind side of the referee and managed to prevent the goalkeeper from getting close to Storer by falling over in the melee and hauling him down in the process. He got lots of praise from the lads for his part in that goal, and once again his experience played a vital part. He could see that the Rovers player could get a block in, so he just blocked him off, which I suppose is technically illegal, but just gave Stuart that split second of space to score. And what a vital goal that was.

We managed to hold on for the win, and at the end we made a dash for the safety of the dressing room. There we discovered Hereford had lost to Leyton Orient, meaning we now only needed a draw in our final game to secure our League status.

Outside and above us the fans were tearing the Goldstone to pieces. While we as a team were delighted to finally be off the bottom of the table, I felt saddened that we'd played the final ever game at the ground. I felt Bill Archer had stitched up the club for no other reason than to make money.

It was a very emotional time for everyone and that situation didn't help the fact that we were preparing now for what was the most important game in the club's history.

We trained as usual in the week leading up to the match with Hereford, and stayed in a hotel away from the town. All week Steve Gritt encouraged us to just go out and play our natural game, saying that everything would turn out fine. The team spirit was terrific and if anyone had seen us in the evenings they would never have guessed we were a bunch of lads who would be playing for our Football League lives on Saturday afternoon. Dave Martin was the instigator of much of the fun, and although he only played the one game for Brighton, he was a brilliant bloke around the dressing room.

I was once again disappointed to be on the bench, but couldn't really argue with Steve Gritt's decision to start with the same eleven who began the game with Doncaster. With both sides knowing that defeat would send them down, there was more tension even than at the Goldstone the previous Saturday. To be honest, I don't remember too much about the early part of the game. It wasn't the best of matches, but we were holding our own until Kerry Mayo deflected a shot past Mark Ormerod to give them the lead. That was a huge blow. Suddenly we were staring at the abyss.

At half-time Steve Gritt was calm as anything – certainly on the outside – and he told us to just continue playing the way we had and a goal would come. Thankfully he was proved absolutely right.

My chance came early on in the second half, when I replaced Paul McDonald, who was struggling a bit with an injury. We were starting to press Hereford back more and I'd been on the pitch less than ten minutes when Craig Maskell hit a beautiful shot from just outside the penalty area that crashed against the far post. Often, the ball will bounce out harmlessly away from the goal or go behind for a corner or goal kick when it's hit the frame of the goal, but you are always told as an attacking player to get into the box and be ready for the one occasion in maybe ten when it will come back out. You have to be on your toes and ready to react and beat opposing defenders to the ball. Fortunately, on this occasion, it bounced straight out to me, and I knew what I had to do. I hit it as hard as I could with my left foot and it hit the back of the net. The fans behind that goal went ballistic!

The next thing I knew I was being mobbed by the team and I heard a voice in my ear say, "Robbie, you just saved my life, mate." Of course, it was Kerry Mayo and I think at the time he meant it and we've since become great mates and see each other fairly regularly – and he invited me to play in his testimonial legends game. I understand what he meant. Can you imagine how he would have felt and how he might have been treated if his deflection had ended up being the goal that sent the club out of the league? It doesn't bear thinking about.

We held out for the final 30 minutes of the game and at the final whistle, I remember pandemonium breaking out amongst the Brighton fans behind the goal. I had been so wrapped up in the match that I hadn't noticed the riot police in full gear ready to come on to the pitch. There were 8,500 people crammed into Hereford's tiny Edgar Street ground, and at that moment it seemed that almost all of them were Brighton. While the team went over to celebrate with the fans, the Police formed a line on the centre circle to keep the two sets of supporters apart.

I really felt for the Hereford lads; they'd given their all and it hadn't been good enough and they were absolutely devastated. We were mentally and physically drained, and when we got back to the dressing room I think it really began to hit us that we had pulled off the great escape. We celebrated with a few beers on the coach on the way back to Brighton, where we were greeted by a few jubilant fans – I think the rest were still celebrating somewhere in Hereford!

The following season was always going to be difficult, playing home games away from Brighton, and I was amazed at how many fans did make the trip to Gillingham to watch us. I was a regular in the side until Steve Gritt was sacked, unfairly in my opinion, given what he'd achieved for us, and the circumstances in which he had to work. Some managers you get on with and some you don't and it was soon clear that I didn't feature in Brian Horton's plans, so it was no surprise when my contract wasn't renewed.

I signed for Leyton Orient and it was quite early in the season when we played Brighton at Brisbane Road. Before the game, I said to the Orient lads, "You watch the reaction when my name is read out." It was quite amusing to see the looks on their faces as the Brighton fans chanted my name. It is fantastic to know that I have a special place in Seagulls fans' hearts.

I played non-league for a while with Stevenage and Maldon, but I haven't played for a while now, and I have a good job on the railways. I may not have achieved what the likes of David Beckham or Wayne Rooney have in their careers, but very few players do. But I am proud of the fact that my goal kept Brighton in the Football League and that people still come up to me in the street and congratulate me for it, even today.

DANNY CULLIP
CENTRE-HALF 1999-2004

BORN   17 September 1976
DEBUT   18 September 1999
ALBION CAREER   242 games, 10 goals

If one player epitomised the spirit the Micky Adams engendered in the club during his first term as Albion manager it was Danny Cullip. A tough, no-nonsense, vocal centre half, who always made life uncomfortable for opposition strikers, he was signed from Brentford for a bargain £50,000 on October 13th 1999, and led the back line superbly through 216 appearances in the five years he spent at Withdean. Scoring a championship-clinching winning goal makes his decision for the match of his life a straight-forward choice.

Brighton & Hove Albion 1 v Chesterfield 0

League Division Three
Tuesday 1 May 2001

Withdean Stadium
Attendance 6,847

*Cullip nets the goal which wins the Division Three championshp
for the Seagulls*

Teams

Micky Adams	Managers	Nicky Laws
Michel Kuipers		Mike Pollitt
Paul Watson		Marcus Ebdon
Danny Cullip		Ian Breckin
Andy Crosby		Chris Beaumont
		(Sub. Daniel Barrett)
Kerry Mayo		Stephen Payne
Paul Rogers		Jon Howard
		(Sub. Luke Beckett)
Richard Carpenter		Jamie Ingledow
Charlie Oatway		Ryan Williams
(Sub. Steve Melton)		
Gary Hart		Greg Pearce
(Sub. Lee Steele)		
Paul Brooker		David Reeves
(Sub. Martin Thomas)		
Bobby Zamora		Rob Edwards
Cullip 78	Goals	

Referee: S Bennett (Kent)

I STARTED OUT AT OXFORD UNTED as a teenager when Denis Smith was the manager and in those days they were still playing at the old Manor Ground. They had a good side and won promotion to what is now the Championship, although I didn't feature in the first team. That summer I made the move to West London to join Fulham, who at that time were in the old Fourth Division, along with the likes of Hull City and Wigan Athletic, who are also now in the Premiership.

Micky Adams had just landed his first managerial role with the club at their lowest ebb, having finished in the bottom half of the table, and at one point looking candidates for relegation to non-league football. Micky was still turning out in those days, although that was his final season as a player. He brought full-back Paul Watson and Darren Freeman from his old club Gillingham, and Richard Carpenter later joined them. All three were proven winners, having helped Gillingham achieve promotion from the same division the previous season. Goalkeeper Mark Walton arrived from Bolton Wanderers and midfielder Paul Brooker was also in the squad, along with former Southampton midfielder Glenn Cockerill.

In 1996/97 we were neck and neck with Wigan and Carlisle for the title, but missed out on the Championship due to a rule change that meant for the first and only time, instead of goal average or goal difference, goals scored were the criteria when clubs were level on points. Fulham had a superior goal difference to Wigan, but the Latics scored 12 more goals than us, which cost us the title. Ironically, it was Jimmy Hill, who was then the Chairman at Craven Cottage, who had been instrumental in pushing through the rule change.

Mohamed Al-Fayed bought the club in the summer of 1997 and within four months Micky was sacked and replaced, famously, by Kevin Keegan. Like a new manager, a fresh owner wants to bring in his own team and this was certainly the case at Fulham. But Micky certainly was never given the money that Keegan and his successor Paul Bracewell had to spend. Looking back, I'm very proud at what we achieved that season, and it was a testament to Micky that the team he put together on a shoestring won promotion. In my opinion we put Fulham back on the footballing map and without that team, who knows if Fayed would have been interested in buying the club?

After a brief spell at Swansea City, Micky was soon back in west London with Brentford and although I had continued to play regularly for Fulham in the first half of the 1997/98 season, he paid £75,000 to take me across to Griffin Park in February 1998 – and I jumped at the chance of linking up with him again, even though the season ended with the Bees being relegated to the Football League's bottom division. Brentford owner Ron Noades decided he could do a better job and took over as the manager, and to make matters even worse I picked a cruciate knee ligament injury early in the campaign, which meant I missed the rest of the season.

I hadn't played a first team game for 13 months when Micky, now in charge at Brighton, took me on a month's loan at Withdean in September 1999 – that was a major show of faith. Micky had only been at the club since April, and during the summer had made wholesale changes to the squad, but there were plenty of familiar faces there when I arrived in September 1999. Darren Freeman, Paul Watson and Mark Walton all started alongside me when I made my debut in the home match against Chester, while a familiar former foe was the club's new captain Paul Rogers, who had played in the Wigan side that had pipped Fulham to the title two years earlier.

That opening game against a struggling side was nothing to write home about, although I did score an equaliser with seven minutes to go. But just when we thought we'd done enough for a point, Chester scored in the dying seconds, to make it a losing debut. We kept clean sheets in the following three matches against Cheltenham Peterborough and Carlisle. I must have impressed in those games as Micky was given the green light to pay Brentford £50,000 to make the move permanent. Having played for him twice before I didn't need asking twice about linking up with him for a third time, and my instinct proved to be a good decision as I enjoyed the best spell of my career with the Albion.

Despite all the new players at the club, Micky was still keen to sign more to give the club a side capable of challenging for promotion. The problem that season was that, although we were good defensively, we were unable to kill teams off. That all changed when, in February 2000, he unearthed Bobby Zamora, who first came on loan from Bristol Rovers. Bobby made an immediate impact, scoring the equaliser in the draw with Plymouth at

Withdean. Bobby followed this up by scoring a further five goals in as many games, including a hat-trick in our 7-1 win at Chester.

We finished the season on a high with a 14 game unbeaten run, but six of those were drawn, otherwise we would have ended the campaign not too far from the play-off places. We had a great bunch of players at the club already, but in the summer Micky put the final pieces of the jigsaw together, bringing in two midfielders, Paul Brooker and Richard Carpenter, both former Fulham colleagues of mine, who had played in the team that had won promotion. Then, two days before the start of the season the club paid Bristol Rovers £100,000 for Bobby Zamora. Nobody took much notice at the time, but having played with Bobby for six games the previous season, everyone at the football club knew that was a massive signing.

When he signed for us Bobby was still a teenager, yet the one thing that impressed, apart from his obvious talent, was his character. Micky always looked into a player's character before signing anyone; he wanted to make sure they would fit into the tight-knit squad. Bobby went straight into the side for our first game of the season at Southend, which I had to sit out through suspension. I can't say I was sorry as the temperature was in the eighties and I was suffering from exhaustion in the dug-out, so goodness knows how the players were feeling out on the pitch. The Brighton fans, as always, turned out in force, but in the end went home disappointed, as we were beaten 2-0 – but defeats proved to be a rarity that season.

I've always said that no matter how much work you do in pre-season, and how many friendly matches you play you do need to play four or five competitive games before you are fully match fit. I made my first appearance of the 2000/01 season in the defeat against Millwall in the League Cup, and then we lost the next two matches against Lincoln and Kidderminster. Having spent a fair bit of money that summer, Micky came under a bit of pressure, and as a group of players we felt our share of responsibility. The boys had a meeting, as we were disappointed with how things were going, especially having finished the previous season in such good form. We wanted to kick on again after that and a lot was aired between the players. Nobody pointed fingers, we didn't argue amongst ourselves, but we worked things out. We knew we were capable of challenging and I think everybody felt much better after that, and we ended up going on a ten-game unbeaten run.

During that spell, Micky's assistant manager Alan Cork left to take charge of one of our Division Three rivals, Cardiff City. Bob Booker came in as Micky's assistant in October. He'd worked with Charlie Oatway, myself and a few of the lads at Brentford and I knew we were getting a good character, who perhaps has never got the credit he's deserved for his role in the club's successes. Bob's a great impressionist. Everybody will remember him dressing up as Freddie Mercury at the end of the second championship season, but he's not there just because he is a good bloke and makes everyone laugh – he's also a very, very good coach, and I'm pleased to see him back at the club working with Micky again.

Our unbeaten run had taken us to second place when we went to Saltergate to play Chesterfield in October. They were top of the table and were paying quite a bit of money in wages for a club in our division, and there were a lot or rumours and stories going around about how they paid they players – but that sort of thing didn't have any affect on us. We just got on with our jobs, and didn't take any notice of it really. I think it rankled more with the fans, what was happening, than it did with the players.

We were more annoyed with the referee after Charlie Oatway got sent off early in the second half of the game, but we defended well and it looked like we were going to take a deserved point from the game, but Jamie Ingledow scored with just about the last kick of the game to win it for them. It was cruel on us (but we would have our revenge) and we bounced back after that and went on another good run. We were virtually unbeatable at Withdean, and lost only one more game there all season. Our away form was also good, so by the time we played Plymouth at Home Park on Easter Saturday we knew that a win could see us seal promotion. Plymouth is a hard place to go and get a result at the best of times, but with the group of characters we had at the club at the time, it was the sort of challenge that we relished. And we had the best start possible when Paul Brooker scored very early on and then Bobby got another about ten minutes later. We held on to win comfortably enough, and with Rochdale only drawing at Macclesfield and Hull beating Hartlepool those results meant we'd won promotion with still half a dozen games of the season left.

Of course, there were celebrations afterwards – and with a bit of the season still to play, they seemed to go on for ever. We got a great reception from the fans at Withdean on Easter Monday with the win over Darlington, but it was the Championship we were after. Chesterfield had led the table for a long time, but we always felt we were a better side than them and we wanted to prove that we were the best side in the division. By the time they arrived at Withdean they'd had their nine points deducted for their financial irregularities and they couldn't catch us. But, everyone involved with the club, from the fans through to the players, didn't want to win the championship by default. To be true champions we were desperate to finish ten points above them, although we knew that we would clinch the title, with or without the nine-point cushion, with victory at Withdean that night. That's all we thought about; we didn't look at them and think about how they'd been paid or what they'd been up to behind the scenes. We just wanted to beat them and win the title.

Night games at Withdean were fantastic and there was always a great atmosphere. The evening of the Chesterfield game was no exception and certainly the banter between the two sets of fans spiced it up a bit. Some Albion fans had brought along a big brown envelope and were passing it along the south stand before the game. Micky is a great motivator, but we didn't need any motivating that night. We just wanted to prove that we were the best team in the league – and when I say team, I mean team. We played a lot of clubs that season that had a group of individual players who were better than us, but as a team collectively they were no match. We were the best unit in the division. You can have the best individual players in the world but if you don't play as a team you won't win anything.

It was a tense game as a lot of these types of matches tend to be, and it looked as if we would have to wait for the title. But, as quite often happens the game was settled a by a set piece. I think it was Kerry Mayo who had a shot from about 25 yards, which their keeper saved to give us a corner. All season Paul Watson's delivery from free-kicks and corners had been spot on. With Watto, you catch his eye while the opposition defenders are getting ready to defend the free kick or corner and before they knew it he could put a quick ball in and catch them totally unaware. Bobby Zamora will tell you he got about a third of his goals in the time he was with us from Watto's free-kicks and corners. They had a telepathic understanding, they literally just needed a glance at each other, and before you knew it Watto had put a quick ball in and Bobby had stuck the ball in the back of the net. Micky has always worked hard on set plays, both attacking and defensive, and once again it worked perfectly against Chesterfield, but this time it was me, not Bobby who was the beneficiary. Watto put the ball exactly where I knew he was going to and I just headed it in. That felt great!

We played out the final ten or fifteen minutes before everyone went crazy as the final whistle blew. The scenes afterwards were brilliant. Winning that game was absolutely outstanding and especially as we were able to pick up the trophy on the night. For us to win the championship outright meant a hell of a lot to us, and the most pleasing thing was that regardless of Chesterfield's points deduction we were still champions.

After that we just had to finish the season. No matter how good a campaign you've had you can lose the last couple of games and it can ruin your summer. As it happened we didn't score another goal in our final two fixtures, drawing 0-0 at Halifax and then losing the final match at Shrewsbury, but I am very proud of what we achieved with that team. I think some fans seem to forget a little bit what that squad of players did for the club. That squad won back-to-back promotions and provided many of those who went on to win a Millennium Stadium final in 2004. It's unlikely our achievements will be matched too often, but you never know how things will turn out.

After the play-off final, I turned down a new contract in December 2004, but to be honest if Micky Adams had still been with the club, there's every chance I would have stayed. At the time Sheffield United were at the top of the Championship and pushing for promotion to the Premiership. They were a massive side and I felt that it was too good an opportunity to miss. I felt if I didn't take the opportunity, I would end up regretting it, and although things didn't work out I don't regret it, as I would have spent the rest of my life wondering what might have happened. I played my last game for Brighton in the 2-0 defeat at Millwall and made my Sheffield United debut against Leicester City the following week.

I was only at Bramall Lane for three months, but I played every single game while I was there. After I signed we had a great run in the league, spoiled by Brighton of all clubs, when they nicked a famous win up there in the last minute. We also had a great FA cup run and I scored the equaliser when we beat Aston Villa 3-1 in the third round. We knocked out West Ham – then in the Championship – in the fourth round and then drew at Highbury against Arsenal. I didn't play in the replay, which we lost on penalties, and I only played two more games for the club before I went out on loan to Watford. I left Bramall Lane not because of my football, it was down to a clash of personalities between Neil Warnock and I. Neil had plenty to say about it in his book, but I would prefer not to say any more on the subject, and let Brighton supporters draw their own conclusions.

I then spent 18 months with Nottingham Forest, before moving on to Queens Park Rangers and Gillingham. If I wanted to I could have carried on playing in League One or League Two this season, but I just decided that I didn't fancy the trek of nearly two hours to training in the morning, or living away from home four nights a week. I'm settled in Sussex with a young family, and I've got my routines and I like to stick to them. After moving to Sheffield and then so quickly to Forest it didn't really suit me to be honest. Now I get to see a lot more of my kids which is good for me, and I'm enjoying the challenge of playing under Kevin Keehan at Lewes

My happiest times of my career were undoubtedly at Brighton & Hove Albion. I'm always at my best when I'm settled, and my time down here was definitely was definitely my most settled and most successful. I've got many happy memories, and I'll never forget the game of my life, when we won the league title at Withdean.

BOBBY ZAMORA
STRIKER 2000–2003

BORN   16 January 1981
DEBUT   12 February 2000
ALBION CAREER   136 games, 83 goals

One of the greatest strikers to wear the stripes, between 2000 and 2003 barely a week passed without Bobby Zamora scoring for the Albion, as he netted 83 goals in 136 appearances, helping the club win back-to-back championships as they rose from the Third to the First Division. A match winner week after week, Bobby set a club record by scoring in ten successive matches on the way to lifting the Second Division Championship in 2001/02.

Brighton & Hove Albion 3 v Reading 1

League Division One
Monday 11 February 2002

Withdean Stadium
Attendance 6,756

Brighton outplay their major rival on their way to the title

Teams

Peter Taylor	Managers	Alan Pardew
Michel Kuipers		Ben Roberts
Robbie Pethick		Graeme Murty
Danny Cullip		John Mackie
Adam Virgo		Adie Williams
Paul Watson		Nicky Shorey
Steve Melton		Sammy Igoe
		(Sub. Jamie Cureton)
Junior Lewis		Andy Hughes
		(Sub. Darius Henderson)
Richard Carpenter		Keith Jones
Paul Brooker		John Salako
Paul Hart		Nicky Forster
Bobby Zamora		Tony Rougier
		(Sub. Neil Smith)
Zamora 60, Melton 64, Lewis 88	Goals	Cureton 90

Referee: P Alcock (Halstead)

IT IS VERY HARD TO pick out one individual match from all those I played for Brighton. It was actually more the case that everything across the whole three years that I was at the club was brilliant – absolutely everything. During the back-to-back championship seasons we hardly lost a game and just seemed to win every week.

There are a few matches which do stand out from my time at the Albion: I remember scoring a hat-trick while I was on loan in 2000 in a 7-1 win at Chester City; I also got trebles against Macclesfield Town and Cambridge United. Then, of course, there was the Chesterfield game when we clinched the Third Division title, but I suppose the one game which stands out above all others is when we beat Reading 3-1 at our place, in February 2002 on the way to the Second Division title.

I didn't know too much about Brighton ahead of my loan switch to the south coast from Bristol Rovers in February 2000. Earlier that season I had gone on loan to Bath City and scored eight goals in six games for them. They wanted me to stay on, but I didn't really want to because I wanted to push on a bit and try and play in the Football League. So I stayed at Bristol Rovers for a couple of months and then the opportunity to join Brighton came along. I was told they wanted to take me on loan and it was a chance to play some regular first-team football.

I said yes straight away. It was ideal for me really. I didn't really know much about the club, but I went down there and it was brilliant from day one. I scored on my debut against Plymouth Argyle and everything just seemed to go on from there. It was great. I remember turning up for my first day at the Falmer training ground and Charlie Oatway saying to me, "Right, let's see what you have got," and that stands out because I thought straight away that he was quite funny.

I was only 18 years old and I didn't really know too much about any of the players. I knew a few names and I'd heard of Micky Adams, but I didn't really know too many faces. It was a whole new world, but it was a brilliant new world. It was so much fun for me to come in and straight away to be made so welcome. It made things so much easier and on the back of all that

I scored six in six – including that hat-trick at Chester City. The Brighton fans took to me straight away and the month was a huge success.

After my loan spell ended I went back to Bristol and Rovers told me that they wanted me back and we would see how I got on, but I didn't get used much. I kept in contact with Micky and Corky [Alan Cork] and they told me that they were thinking about putting a bid in and that they would speak to Rovers and see what the initial reaction was.

I was quite lucky that the youth coach at Bristol Rovers Phil Bater was a very good guy and he had always looked out for me, as much as the club. He told me that Brighton had put an offer in for me and that Ian Holloway, the manager, wanted to see me. I think he had already had a chat with the manager and Phil told me that he didn't want me to go – but he also said that it was a chance for me to play first team football at Brighton and that if I wanted to go there then I should just be strong and tell the manager that. After that chat I just thought, "yes, I'll go for it."

Ian Holloway is quite a character, but he is also quite a tough bloke, particularly if you are a young player coming through. As a young pro it was quite hard to stand up to him and tell him I wanted to leave his club. In fact I found it hard to say too much at all to him. Phil picked up on the vibes beforehand and said, "I'm going to come in with you, so you can say what you want to say and not be scared. You get one chance and you need to bite the bullet and tell him."

So I went in to the manager's office and told him that I wanted to go and Olly said, "no, I don't want you to go. I think you will play a few games here for us this season."

But then Phil did me a favour by stepping up and saying, "I don't want you to do that, that is out of order, you should let him go. He's not going to get that many games here – you know that."

In the end Olly said, "okay, fair enough. If that is what you want then I will let you go."

I will always be grateful to Phil that he was there and said those things for me. I'm very grateful to Olly too for giving me the chance to join Brighton. He didn't have to sell me, and I think he liked me as a player, but the situation was that he had some very good forwards there at the time, including Nathan Ellington and Jamie Cureton, who have gone on to great things, and I felt I would have just been on the fringe again that season without really playing much. Now I was really looking forward to playing first-team football.

Brighton paid £100,000 for me. Looking back, it was a lot of money for someone with my limited experience and it was a big gamble for Micky Adams and the club to take. I am really grateful that they did, but at the time, without wanting to sound blasé, I don't think it really meant that much to me. All my mates who I had grown up playing football with in London – such as John Terry, Jay-Lloyd Samuel, Ledley King and Paul Konchesky – were all playing in the Premiership and at that age they were probably on wages of around £12,000 a week and so in that context £100,000 did not seem that big a deal to me.

I now realise, knowing the club, knowing the division and knowing football, that for Brighton to pay £100,000 for me was a huge sum at the time – but I don't think the money thing ever really came into my head at that point. To me it wasn't millions like the amount being spent on transfers such as £7 million for Carl Cort to go to Newcastle or £13 million for Robbie Keane to join Inter Milan as also happened that summer, and so that meant it did not seem a lot of money. I was young and naïve about the transfer business and club finances and so I didn't really think about it at all. It only really sunk in half-way through the first season that Micky had risked so much on me and that it was a big deal. But thankfully by then it wasn't a burden because I was scoring goals.

I had a great relationship with Micky Adams. He was the first manager to give me the chance to play regular football and he was desperate for me to do well. He took the gamble and so it was on his head, so I guess he would have been very pleased that I came good and scored a few goals early in my Brighton career.

It wasn't long before a lot of clubs were interested and sending scouts to come and see me and, while I was never tapped up, there are always ways for clubs to let a player know they are interested and there were intimations that I could get a lot more money – five or six times what Brighton were paying me at the time – but I wasn't really interested in that. I was already in the same division as the clubs that were interested and I was really happy at Brighton. The lads were brilliant and the thought of moving was never in my head. I never once banged on Micky's door, or the chairman's door for more money. As I say I wasn't interested in that at all, I just wanted to stay at Brighton and wasn't interested in a sideways move just for a few more quid.

At the end of the first season we won the first of the back-to-back championships and that was just awesome really. For me to play my first season, score a lot of goals and then be part of the team that won the championship was incredible. We were playing football in a brilliant style as well. We weren't one of those teams that just bangs it up front and we had a great understanding as a group of players. We all knew when someone had the ball exactly where they were going to put it. Every player knew exactly where the other one would be and I had a particularly good understanding with Paul Watson. Whenever Watto got the ball I knew precisely where I needed to run to and he knew where to deliver it to. It was just such a great connection: Watto has an absolutely wonderful left foot and it made my job as a striker so much easier when you get deliveries like that. Even now, having spent a few seasons playing in the Premiership, I don't think I have come across anybody with a better left foot than Watto's. In the current Fulham team there isn't anybody with a better delivery than Watto at his peak. I was very lucky to have played in the same team as him: he created numerous goals for me; not only with his deliveries but with his intelligent play as well.

It's hard to pick out individuals from that era – Paul Rogers, Charlie Oatway, Richard Carpenter and Danny Cullip stand out for their obvious qualities, and Nathan Jones and Paul Brooker were great out wide. Not only did those two do my running for me, but they were good friends off the pitch too! But to be honest I could go through absolutely every player who played over those two seasons. The whole squad were absolutely brilliant and I wouldn't want to leave anybody out. A lot of people said without me Brighton were nothing, but that was rubbish. We had some superb players throughout the side. I remember being suspended at Colchester as we closed in on the Second Division championship in 2002 and I sat in the stand and watched the team absolutely annihilate Colchester 4-1.

Paul Brooker arrived at the same time as I did and we got on very well. Jonesey is also a great character and a great lad, but every single one of us at the club got on famously well on and off the pitch. There were obviously the occasional flare-ups and bits and pieces from time to time, but that is just competitive football and the fire inside some of the characters that we had at the club, but we had a great togetherness because we all wanted to do well and we wanted to win things.

After that first championship, everybody outside the club felt the next season was going to be all about survival, but we just carried on where we had left off in the Third Division. We continued playing brilliant football, dominated teams and won the Championship again – which was absolutely brilliant. It is a very rare thing for any club to win back-to-back titles of any description, so for us to do so in two different divisions was a fantastic achievement indeed.

We lost Micky early on in the following season. He got tapped up and being a greedy so-and-so, he went for the money! In truth, a bigger club came in and it was a chance for him to take that step up to the Premiership with Leiecster City. He took it and thankfully another good manager in Peter Taylor came in straight away to take over. That was fortunate for us. Some people say Peter just inherited Micky's team, but you still have to manage the players well and that is something that has to be done on a daily basis. If Peter had wanted to, he could have got rid of people and brought his own men in but he kept the lads that were here and carried on where Micky had left off. Yes, we were Micky's players, but Peter still had a lot to do. He had to coach us, manage the team and pick the side. He kept the lads motivated and he did that extremely well as can be seen by the fact that we won the championship.

The home game with Reading in the February of 2002 was probably the turning point. I remember it was one of those special Withdean nights. It was a Monday night, bucketing down with rain. Ahead of the game Reading were seven points ahead of us at the top of the table, but we beat them emphatically.

I think we got into their heads the fact that we were chasing them, that we were better than them, that we were going to beat them whatever it took. Football is a mental game, as well as a physical game and defeats like that take their toll on players. We dominated them, bashed them up and then humiliated them in the way we won 3-1 that night. I think that knocked them down a peg or two.

We blew them away in the second half, I scored after about an hour. I remember Paul Brooker set me up with a back-heel and I cut inside from a tight angle, took a couple of touches and smashed the ball past Ben Roberts.

Four minutes later, Steve Melton added a second. I remember our three midfielders – Richard Carpenter, Junior Lewis and Melts – played superbly that night. We went two up when Melts made a brilliant run from midfield. I chipped a ball over the defence for him and he scored a brilliant lob. Junior added the third when we broke with only a couple of minutes left. I went around the keeper and slid the ball across the face of goal and left him with a tap in on his debut. It was a superb performance, and even my old Bristol Rovers team-mate Jamie Cureton's late consolation couldn't take the gloss off a great night's work. After that we only lost once more that season – away at Stoke City, who also won promotion – as we turned up the heat on Reading and eventually overhauled them to win the title with a game to spare.

Those two seasons are right up there with everything else that I have subsequently achieved in football. It was a phenomenal achievement and as far as memories go I don't think that can be beaten. The subsequent season in the championship under Martin Hinshelwood and then Steve Coppell was equally brilliant – even if we did eventually get relegated. Again everybody wrote us off before a ball was even kicked, but we took the fight to the final game. At times it was a little frustrating on a personal level. After winning at Burnley and drawing with Coventry, I got injured in the third game against Norwich at home and I was out for a while with a knee injury. It was extra frustrating because we had started off so well with that emphatic win at Burnley on the first day of the season. We then had that hideous run of 13 successive defeats, but we did brilliantly to come back from that in the second half of the season and nearly rescue ourselves.

It was a tough season, but one that I thoroughly enjoyed. We were rubbing shoulders with teams that had much bigger resources than us, so to go right down to the wire for a club that has just come up was brilliant. I think that, in all honesty, we probably should have stayed in that division. I think with a bit more belief we could have done it – unfortunately we didn't – but I loved the experience.

Had we stayed up then possibly I might have stayed for another season. It is difficult to know how things might have panned out if we had stayed in that division. One thing I wanted to do was to keep going forward and returning to the Second Division might not have worked out for me.

I love the club, though, and I didn't want to leave and just go anywhere for any old sake, which is why I was never interested in going to Wigan Athletic or Cardiff City at a time when they were in the same division as Brighton – but when the move to Spurs came along, it was too good an opportunity to turn down and, while things didn't turn out how I would have liked, I thoroughly enjoyed my time at Tottenham.

Football has a fair bit of politics, and at times it can be about whether your face fits. Glenn Hoddle had signed me and then he got sacked not long afterwards. David Pleat took charge and we didn't really see eye-to-eye, but the lads there were brilliant and I learned so much from my time there. I took a chance by stepping back down to the Championship with West

Ham, but it was the opportunity of playing regular football again that was the pull for me. Added to that, West Ham were my boyhood team, the team I supported growing up, and it was just the right time for me to do that. I wanted to go there and do well, but there were some ups and downs. Losing in the Play-off final was a down, but then a year later I got the winning goal in the final and that was a dream come true for me.

I left both Spurs and West Ham because you can only sit on the bench or twiddle your thumbs in the stand for so long. You want to be playing football and you miss that. After the buzz of going out Saturday after Saturday and winning with Brighton, playing well week-in, week-out, it is hard when you are not playing every game. When I signed for Tottenham I thought it was great and I didn't really think it would be that different to life at Brighton – so it doesn't really hit you until you are there that you are not playing every week. But going to Tottenham and seeing and learning what I did was invaluable. Then going to West Ham and playing some football, taking it slowly again and gradually creeping up and learning more allowed me to re-establish myself as a Premiership player.

In 2008 I switched from Upton Park to Craven Cottage and at the time of writing I am loving being at Fulham – largely because I am playing every week again. But one day I would love to come back to Brighton and play for the Albion again. I always tell my mates that I will go back there at some point in the future, but when I do come back Dick Knight will need to make sure there is a decent team behind me, just as there was the first time!

CHARLIE OATWAY
MIDFIELD 1999-2007

BORN   28 November 1973
DEBUT   7 August 1999
ALBION CAREER   248 games, 9 goals

Charlie Oatway joined the Albion from Brentford in 1999 as one of Micky Adams' first signings for the club. Prior to his spell at Griffin Park he had played for Torquay United and Cardiff City, having been spotted playing non-league soccer at Yeading, but the most successful part of his career came during his time with Brighton. He played almost 250 games for the club, scored nine goals, helped the club to three promotions, and captained the Albion at the Millennium Stadium.

Brighton & Hove Albion 1 v Bristol City 0

League Division One Play-off final
Sunday 30 May 2004

Millennium Stadium
Attendance 65,167

The Albion win promotion on the biggest stage of all

Teams

Mark McGhee	Managers	Danny Wilson
Ben Roberts		Steve Phillips
Guy Butters		Brian Carey
Danny Cullip		Tony Butler
		(Sub. Mark Goodfellow)
Adam Virgo		David Coles
Dan Harding		Matthew Hill
Charlie Oatway		Tony Rougier
Nathan Jones		Tom Doherty
(Sub. John Piercy)		
Richard Carpenter		Brian Tinnion
(Sub. Paul Reid)		(Sub. Luke Wilkshire)
Gary Hart		Craig Woodman
Leon Knight		Lee Miller
		(Sub. Scott Murray)
Bobby Zamora		Tony Roberts
Knight pen 84	Goals	

Referee: R Beeby (Northamptonshire)

I WAS LUCKY ENOUGH TO BE part of three fantastic promotion-winning sides during my time as a player at the Albion. The back-to-back championships in 2001 and 2002 were fantastic achievements – easily the best of my career – but asked to select the match of my life it is undoubtedly the 2004 Play-off final win over Bristol City at the Millennium Stadium which stands out. It was the only time in my career that I encountered the end-of-season play-offs and it is a magnificent way to win promotion. You start the season wanting to be champions, but for pure feel-good factor, going up via the play-offs is unrivalled.

The season 2003/04 was an indifferent one for us. After suffering relegation from the old Division One the previous campaign, we had started strongly under Steve Coppell – he was a very quiet man, but an absolutely brilliant manager. I played under a lot of very good managers – particularly at Brighton – but Steve was the best. His preparation for games was unrivalled and he really knew how to bring the best out of players. I think had he stayed that season, then we would have gone up as champions – but he was given the opportunity to manage at Reading, and it was understandable when he left. That said, I know he agonised over the decision and was torn between Brighton and Reading; it wasn't quite as cut-and-dried as it seemed at the time.

Steve's departure hit us hard and our results suffered for a few weeks, but once Mark McGhee arrived we picked up again and, thanks to a brilliant end-of-season run in, we very nearly sneaked into the automatic promotion places. In the end a fourth-placed finish meant it was to be the play-offs and a two-legged tie with fifth-placed Swindon Town. They had a very strong team that season with the likes of Tommy Mooney, Sam Parkin and Rory Fallon in attack, and we knew we would be in for a tough tie. A lot of people said that we got battered in both those games – but that was totally untrue. We had a formation and a way we were going to play away from home in the first leg and it worked. We absorbed a lot of pressure and then Richard Carpenter managed to get a goal and everything worked out as planned in that first away game – but at home we didn't play anywhere near as well as we knew we could play.

The plan in both matches was to make it as difficult as possible for them. Swindon were a good side and capable of beating us, as they had done once already that season, but we had made a habit of making it difficult for teams. We hadn't conceded a goal in nine matches and we wanted to carry on with that run. Not to extend that club record, but because we were at a stage at which we knew that two clean sheets would surely be enough to get us through the semi-finals.

We wanted to try and frustrate them, shut them out, knowing with the attacking players we had in the team – the likes of Leon Knight, Chris Iwelumo, Gary Hart, Nathan Jones, Richard Carpenter – that there was always an opportunity that we would nick a goal. It worked in the first leg, but at home we didn't play as well as we were capable. Nonetheless our grit and determination – and that never-say-die attitude which ran through the team eventually helped us through by the skin of our teeth. Swindon scored to take the game to extra-time and then took the lead – but Adam Virgo, through sheer determination, managed to get what was an unforgettable goal in the last minute. That took us to penalties.

It's funny because I'm not one for scoring goals or anything like that, but I am always one to stand up and be counted. I have had to do that throughout my career. However, during the last ten minutes of the second half of the extra-time I was getting cramp – everywhere. I literally couldn't even run. I recall the boys giving each other rub downs to ease the cramp before the penalty shoot-out. I said to the boss "if I'm needed I'll take one," as simple as that; I had no problem with taking a kick. Score or miss, I would have brushed it off as soon as I had taken it. I put myself up there, but there were five other players willing to take it and the gaffer opted for them.

We had practiced penalties an awful lot in the build up to the semi-final – and again for the final – we went through a stage where the boys were just taking penalties, practicing enough to get into good habits when taking spot-kicks. Mark McGhee told everyone, "I don't mind if you miss – just as long as you do what you've been doing in training."

We each got into our own individual routine – place it to the left, smash it down the middle, side foot it to the right – and the onus was on the player to stick to their routine. That was excellent management by Mark, as it took away the uncertainty in each player's mind as he walked up to take the kick. Mark was good like that. He tried to cover every angle, every eventuality and that way of approaching the shoot-out was really beneficial to us as we won through.

Bristol City were massive favourites to win the final and I think that suited us, but we had a very strong team full of good players and strong characters who had been together for a number of seasons: Danny Cullip, Richard Carpenter, Nathan Jones, Gary Hart. They were brought to the club as Micky Adams laid good foundations shortly after he took over in 1999. Subsequent managers benefited from those foundations, and they were still strong for the Play-off final. When Micky had brought in those players and his assistant Bob Booker, who also remained as number two to Coppell and McGhee, he also instilled a never-say-die attitude in the players and the club and that too served us well in Cardiff.

And with that we didn't care that we were being labeled underdogs, the poor relations. In fact we were pleased to be so. It suited us down to the ground. I'm not sure that it suited Bristol City to be favourites, but you got the feeling they felt it did. That was them all over at that time: they were very casual, very laid back, almost as if they had a right to be there and it was a formality for them to win the game. That said, to be fair to Bristol City, they knew they were in for a tough game. We had played them three or four weeks before that and drew 0-0 at their place, so they knew it was going to be a difficult game and that we were not going to turn up and just roll over for them.

We had the type of players at the club who were not flamboyant or anything like that, but hard working and ready to roll up their sleeves up and get on with it. Even those who had come in since the back-to-back championships – the likes of Chris Iwelumo, Ben Roberts, Paul Reid, Leon Knight – had settled in quickly and shared the group's mentality. Much has been said and written about Leon and his attitude – and I didn't like hearing some of the rubbish that came from him after he left the club – but in that season he was superb for us. He scored 27 goals and when it mattered in Cardiff he showed a huge amount of bottle and character to step up to the plate and take that late penalty kick which eventually won us the final.

The hotel we stayed at was in the centre of Cardiff overlooking the bay. In the build-up to and aftermath of the game I filmed a DVD diary, which the club then sold to supporters – it was another diversionary thing to take all our minds off the importance of the game. I also remember locking Dan Harding out of his bedroom, out on the balcony! He didn't like heights, but that was one of the funniest points of the whole weekend and helped take people's minds off the match. Dan was nearly crying and ended up desperately phoning people to get them to come up to his room and unlock the door, but when I had tricked him out there I had locked the door and hidden the key. I think he was out there for about half an hour!

The Play-off final was the biggest single game of my career and I would be lying if I didn't say I wasn't nervous. I think most players get nervous for any senior game. People know that I'm a constant Mickey-taker; some people think that I do that for other people's benefit, but if I'm honest I do that just as much for myself to calm my own nerves. No matter what level you play at as a pro you have a lot of pressure on yourself. You're providing for your families. I take the Mickey to pass the time and keep everyone, including myself, happy and smiling.

After the incident with Dan Harding, and he had seen the funny side of it, we had a team meal and a brief chat before getting our heads down for night – or at least that was then plan! At that time it was all the Play-off finals over one weekend, and on the day before our game West Ham played Crystal Palace. We had loads of Palace and West Ham fans in our hotel and I'm sure it was some Palace fans who kept ringing the room I was sharing with Richard Carpenter. They kept us up all night. We couldn't unplug the phone, so we asked reception at two or three o'clock in the morning if they could put a trace on the calls and get it dealt with, but they said they couldn't do that, and they couldn't change the room because the hotel was fully booked, so we had a night of being woken up by the phone ringing at regular intervals.

When you go down for breakfast on the morning of a game, one of the first concerns of any manager is, "have you slept well, are you okay?" Chippy [Richard Carpenter] near enough bit Mark McGhee's head off when he asked the question. So, Chippy and I hadn't had the best preparation for the game. I think a couple of fans must have seen us walking out of our room at the hotel. Or perhaps a Bristol City fan got our room number. My money was on a Palace fan. Whoever was behind it, I was pretty tired and a bit brassed off, but once we got going to the stadium the adrenalin began to kick in; even thinking about it now, the hairs on the back of my neck still stand up. On the short coach journey I made sure the boys were all happy and settled, and there was a little bit of banter flying around to ease the tension, but on every matchday, whatever game it is – pre-season, league match, cup tie – I get to a stage in the day when there is no more taking the Mickey. It stops because we're there for business.

I don't think anyone can say anything bad about Mark McGhee's time at the club. He did a very good job in difficult circumstances and I liked him as a man and a manager. He was always very good with his pre-match team talks, but his Millennium Stadium team talk was exceptional even by his standards. One little thing that he did was write up two lists of stadiums and teams on the board in the dressing room. One list had the teams we could be playing against if we won – West Ham, Sunderland, Nottingham Forest – and one list of the teams in the league we were already playing – Colchester, Chesterfield and Torquay. It was a no contest!

It sounds simple. Perhaps even common sense, and something that the players shouldn't even need to be told, but it is those little things, such as seeing it there written in front of you, that give you that bit extra and help you win games. Things come together in football, and those little bits and pieces like that can make the difference between winning and losing. Mark was very good at trying giving you that extra bit – not settling for what he's got, but going the extra step.

I remember he didn't have to say too much to Richard Carpenter and me: just that we had to get close to their central midfield players and get in their faces. Both Brian Tinnion and Tom Doherty were ball players and were very good at that – our job was to stop them. Chippy and I knew the ways and means of how to beat them, and they knew a lot about us and probably knew how we'd go out there and play. With the aid of scouting networks, television, modern football is like that, you know your opposition's strengths and weaknesses and there should be very little that surprises the modern player if they've prepared correctly and we always did that.

Once the team talk was finished it was a case of going out there ready for business. To be honest when we came out of the tunnel the noise that the 65,000 crowd made didn't really hit me. It only really hit me when we scored and that was strange to be stood in the middle of the stadium with noise coming from one end and silence at the other, that really was an odd experience.

The game was horrible. I don't think it was much of a spectacle for the fans, but I didn't care, we were there to do a job and we did it well. I remember at the hotel afterwards one of my family said it was a bad game and I half lost my rag with them. I asked them what they had wanted me to do. Flick the ball over my head, do sixteen kick ups, then smack it up the other end of the pitch. It wasn't about that, it was about my doing the job to the best of our ability and winning. I think at that point I was still overwhelmed by the result. I knew I'd done my job and I think most of the Brighton fans couldn't care less about the quality of the game – only the result.

As the match wore on with the score 0-0 the more I felt we had about us, the more we grew mentally strong and the more chance we had of winning – especially with big Chris Iwelumo and Leon Knight up front. On the day I think that Bristol City just expected it to happen whereas we didn't. We arrived prepared to work for promotion. As the minutes ticked by, I thought 'we've got these beaten.' Their two boys in the middle of the park were going sideways and not making any progress because we were working so hard and the forwards were not getting any joy from Danny Cullip and Guy Butters.

Then came the moment. Chris Iwelumo created the penalty by driving into the box, exchanging passes with Leon Knight and then getting fouled by Danny Coles, who was trying to stop Chris scoring as he was just about to pull the trigger.

Leon kept his cool and scored the penalty, placing it low to Steve Phillips' right hand side. I can remember how I reacted when it went in: it wasn't much of a celebration. I just clenched my fist, but as Leon prepared to take the kick my thoughts were not on the prize, it was on making sure we were okay at the back if he missed. I wasn't thinking of how I was going react if we score. Once it hit the back of the net – and as Leon showed real bottle to take that kick so late in the game – we had to forget about it, forget about the goal. I was saying to everyone, "we've done f**k all yet. Do your individual jobs for the next five minutes and then there will be plenty of time to celebrate afterwards."

The first thing I did on the final whistle was to go to every Bristol City player and shake their hand. I am not sure if that meant a thing to them, but I think there is nothing worse when people get too hyped up over what they have just achieved, especially when it means you have failed and you have them in your faces. The City players have got careers, families and livelihoods and they tried they're best. I know if we'd lost it would have hurt and I would have taken my hat off to anyone who did that to me, so I went round all of their players and also shook hands with their manger Danny Wilson. He patted me on the back and said, "well done Charlie, you got what you deserved." That meant a lot. There is a lot of banter that goes on between teams in the season, but I think all footballers have a mutual respect for their fellow professionals.

After the game we went to the Jury's hotel to meet family and friends and we had some food and a few drinks. The club had laid on a coach for our loved ones, but we ended up with a few extras on the team bus, with people sat in the aisles and kids on adults' laps. I remember Mark McGhee just saying "so what" and allowing us to set off for Brighton with the bus stacked up like that and that meant a lot to the players to be with their families on the way home.

The next season we kicked off in the Championship and in my opinion matched the promotion achievements by staying there, especially with such a limited playing budget. The following season we weren't quite as lucky. That went for me in particular. I suffered a broken ankle in a match against QPR on Boxing Day 2005. Sadly I never played for the club again after that, but the chairman offered me a job working as a community liaison officer, a role I now combine with the post as assistant manager at Havant & Waterlooville. It's great to still be involved with the club on a day-to-day basis, but I'm sure whatever I might achieve in the game in the future, nothing will beat that game at the Millennium Stadium.

GUY BUTTERS
MIDFIELDER 2000-2008

BORN 30 October 1969
DEBUT 31 August 2002
ALBION CAREER 212 games, 9 goals

Central defender Guy Butters began his career with Spurs in the 1980s, before moving to Portsmouth and subsequently on to Gillingham, where he competed in two Play-off finals, one victory one defeat. He arrived at Brighton in the twilight of his professional career just after the Albion had won promotion to the old Division One, having lifted the Second Division championship in 2002. Voted as Player of the Season in 2004, Guy became a popular figure with the Albion fans and it's the final match of the 2004/05 Championship season which Guy selects as his Albion Match of My Life.

Brighton & Hove Albion 1 v Ipswich Town 1

League Division One
Sunday 8 May 2005

Withdean Stadium
Attendance 6,848

Brighton avoid relegation with a bit of grit and a lot of determination

Teams

Mark McGhee	Managers	Joe Royle
Alan Blayney		Kelvin Davis
Adam El-Abd		Fabian Wilnis
		(Sub. Drissa Diallo)
		(Sub. Jamie Scowcroft)
Guy Butters		Jason De Vos
Paul Reid		Richard Naylor
Ben Harding		David Unsworth
Gary Hart		Jim Magilton
(Sub. Chris McPhee)		
Charlie Oatway		Tommy Miller
Richard Carpenter		Ian Westlake
Leon Knight		Darren Currie
(Sub. Jake Robinson)		(Sub. Pablo Counago)
Dean Hammond		Marcus Bent
Adam Virgo		Shefki Kuqi
Virgo 10	Goals	Kuqi 4

Referee: M Jones (Chester)

I JOINED THE ALBION IN THE old Division One during Martin Hinshelwood's short time in charge of the club. Over the years Hinsh has been an excellent servant to the club as assistant manager, director of youth and caretaker boss – and he was a good manager. He is a good football man and knows his stuff, but I think it is fair to say when he stepped up to the job as manager, everything that could go against him, did go against him. He was already up against it when he took the job, due to the club's limited resources at that level, brought about by the ongoing stadium issue, but he wasn't helped as the club suffered with injuries to key players.

I made my debut under Hinsh against one of my former clubs Portsmouth at Fratton Park. We played some good football on the day and even led 2-1 at one stage, but we didn't get the rub of the green, losing Graham Barrett to a red card in the second half and ended up beaten 2-4 against the eventual champions. That set the tone for the early part of my Albion career. Things just were not going our way. A 0-1 defeat at Millwall brought another silly sending off, this time for my old Pompey teammate Robbie Pethick; while a home game with another former club, Gillingham, epitomised our start to the season. We gifted them two goals within the space of 60 seconds and found ourselves 2-0 down after just 12 minutes. We rallied, played some good football to pull it back to 2-3 – but then Andy Peterson made a real howler late in the game when he stumbled on a back pass. That was how our luck was going, and after narrow defeats to Stoke City and Rotherham – a game in which Alan Lee was about half a mile offside when he scored the only goal – I was left out of the side to concentrate on building up my fitness. I hadn't had the best pre-season campaign, and I was not firing on all cylinders – but I was at a new club, who were struggling and I wanted to play my part.

By the time I came back into the side Martin Hinshelwood had moved upstairs into a Director of Football role, but I will always be grateful to him for bringing me to Brighton. Steve Coppell had now been appointed manager and for his first match in charge I was paired at centre-half with Adam Virgo, who was 19 years old at the time, for a home game with promotion candidates Sheffield United. We'd lost ten in a row ahead of the game, but the change of manager sparked us into life and the match started well for us. With our talismanic striker Bobby Zamora back from injury we stormed into a 2-0 lead – thanks to goals from Gary Hart and Barrett – and we played some good football at Withdean that afternoon – but that isn't what people remember. We were still two up after 70 minutes, but Sheffield came back at us with four goals in the last 20 minutes to win the game 4-2. Michael Brown scored first and then Carl Asaba scored a 12-minute hat-trick, with goals on 77, 86 and 88. I don't know if it was nerves, a lack of confidence and self belief, whether we just ran out of steam, or a combination of all three, but it was a devastating blow. The dressing room was a grim place after that game, and it got even grimmer the following week as we went down 5-0 at bitter rivals Crystal Palace. I didn't play any part in that game, and although I didn't know it at the time, my Albion season was already over.

After just one game under Steve Coppell, Adam Virgo and I were dropped and banished to the reserves. Bearing in mind the team had played pretty well for the opening 70 minutes of the game against Sheffield United, it appeared Steve had made his mind up about the pair of us during that horrific last 20 minutes. Even at that relatively early stage of the season he needed miracles to get the club out of trouble and he soon brought a few of his own players in. It began to look as if neither Adam nor I had much of a future with the club. Virgo went on loan to Exeter City that season – and very nearly signed a three-year deal with the Devon club – and I spent the final part of the season out on loan at Barnet. Under Steve's guidance, the team was making a real fight of it in the Division One relegation battle; by the spring of 2003 they were in with a realistic shout of staying up. I had a year left on my contract, but I felt it was unlikely that I would play much part the following season whatever division the club was playing, and I was gearing up to hang my boots up at the end of the 2003/04 season. At least one supporter hoped that day would come sooner, as he put me up for sale on an internet auction site during the summer as a 'hardly-used centre-half'!

I've taken a bit of stick during my career – usually about my size – so in all honesty it didn't really bother me that much, but I don't think my family liked it and my team-mates were also fuming! Mind you I was more worried about the fact that I didn't even achieve the reserve price of a fiver!!

By then the club had lost its relegation battle on the final day of the season, going down after a 2-2 draw at Grimsby Town, which meant

Division Two football. However, early the following season my luck began to improve. I got a decent pre-season under my belt and when the club suffered a few injuries at the start of the campaign, I was called up for an early-season home game with Luton – which we won 2-0. I then scored in a 3-3 draw at Plymouth the following week, and again a few weeks later at Rushden & Diamonds. We were right at the top of the division and going very well, but then out of the blue, Steve Coppell left for Reading.

Mark McGhee replaced him as boss, and looking back that proved a watershed in my career. Mark was a real breath of fresh air as manager. Straight away he helped me with a special diet and fitness programme aimed at improving my general match fitness, but more importantly, helping me work towards prolonging my professional football career. He was the first manager to do that and under his guidance I began to thrive and really enjoy my football again. It's fair to say we had an up-and-down winter period, but we found our feet again after Christmas and Mark also recalled Adam Virgo from the wilderness and made some astute signings to bolster the squad and our promotion chances. We maintained our form through to the end of the season and with Leon Knight in superb goal-scoring form we clinched a play-off place. Victory on penalties against Swindon in the semi-finals was a sweet moment – and the 1-0 win in the final against Bristol City was an unbelievable feeling. We'd worked really hard to get to that final, but the real hard work would be in staying in the newly-formed Championship.

The season after we were promoted via the play-offs we knew it was always going to be difficult. Those players who had been involved in 2002/03 knew the finances dictated we were one of the division's poor relations, and to stay up it would be down to a lot of hard graft and effort on the players' behalf. It was the first year of the Championship having that name and pretty much everybody had written us off, once again, before we'd even kicked a ball. Thinking back there was also a little bit of confidence lacking in the team considering we hadn't really made any major signings over the summer. We'd bought in four players, all of whom were unproven at that level, but Darren Currie and Alexis Nicolas did eventually prove astute signings.

When the beginning of the season came I felt fitter than I had ever been. I worked hard on Mark's new fitness regime that summer and during pre-season. However, the team, without much new impetus, was still very inexperienced at this level with a lot expected from young players such as Adam Virgo and Dan Harding, who had been tremendous for the club the previous season, but were still fairly fresh out of youth sides. At the beginning of the season it took us a while to get going, and there were a few too many poor shows – we were suffering in the same way we had two years previously. But once we eventually managed to find our feet we quickly realised we were very good at holding on to clean sheets. We knew if we could nick the odd goal here and there, with the defence holding firm, then we could do well and ultimately stay in the division.

The most famous use of that tactic during that season was when we played West Ham at Upton Park, which was a very memorable day, as I scored the winner. We had needed a big striker up front to help take a bit of pressure off the rest of the team by holding the ball up, and Virgo had been drafted up there early in the season and had done a brilliant job, nicking the vital goal in a televised 1-0 smash-and-grab win at Leicester, and then clinching a point a week later with a late equaliser at Watford. He then grabbed the winner in a 1-0 win over Leeds United at Withdean.

Going into the West Ham game we had signed veteran striker Steve Claridge a couple of days beforehand; he was knocking on the door of 40 at the time. We were obviously under resourced compared with West Ham, who had recently dropped out of the Premier League. We went into the game with an ageing loan player and central defender as our strike force, and lost our inspirational skipper Danny Cullip just before kick-off as he had a virus and threw up all over the floor in the dressing room. It wasn't the most ideal preparation, but the smash-and-grab technique that we had mastered worked remarkably well again as we came away with a famous 1-0 win.

We weathered the storm of wave after wave of home attacks in the first half, and with the 30,000 crowd getting more and more impatient and agitated we sensed we could maybe nick something from the game. With about 20 minutes remaining we won a corner and, after a quick one-two with Steve Claridge, Richard Carpenter sent over a pinpoint cross which I headed into the net right in front of a few thousand Albion fans in the away end at Upton Park – what a fantastic moment.

The Hammers ended up having 17 shots on goal in the game, but just three of them on target, and Marlon Harewood whacked the ball against the post. I remember Michel Kuipers pulling off a good save from a cracking Matthew Etherington effort. The Hammers' frustration boiled over after we scored and Hayden Mullins got in a scrap with Adam Virgo, which ended up with both of them being sent off. I think that incident killed the game as all the steam went from them and we hung on well for victory. Most match reports said we had mugged West Ham and that we'd scored from our one and only chance. Well, yes we did, but football is about scoring goals and not letting them in. It's who scores the most goals that wins, not who plays the best or has the most shots. We scored, they didn't. Simple!

We managed to drag that same smash-and-grab technique into a lot of games that season, and when you look back at the results, all of our wins were by one goal – either 1-0 or 2-1 – and we never scored three in a game. We also pulled off some impressive results, picking up four points off West Ham and Leeds United, and we beat eventual champions Sunderland 2-1 at home.

At the end of February we beat Millwall 1-0 and that put us in 15th place, with a ten-point gap between ourselves and the drop zone – but we then suffered our worst run of the season, losing six on the spin. The last of those defeats came at Preston, where we went down 3-0 and with just five games left to play we had been dragged back into the relegation places. A 1-1 draw with Leicester at Withdean a few days later arrested the slump and we followed that with further draws against Burnley (a match memorable for Mark McCammon's refusal to play the second half, which eventually led to him being told to find his own way home) and West Ham. We were still in the bottom three, but with the teams above us playing each other, we knew a win at already-relegated Rotherham would put our destiny in our own hands. An own goal after 19 minutes proved enough, meaning we went into the Ipswich match knowing a point would be enough to ensure we survived.

I remember staying in a hotel before that vital last match of the season, which was unusual for a home game. Darren Currie had begun the season as an Albion player, after we had signed him from Wycombe Wanderers on a free transfer, but before Christmas he'd left to join Ipswich for £250,000. I remember Mark McGhee telling us before the game, "I don't want you to speak to the Ipswich players. I know you're obviously friends with Darren Currie, but I don't want you to talk to him."

On the morning of the game we were all out walking through town to stretch our legs and we bumped into the Ipswich players, who needed to win to be in with a chance of automatic promotion. We had a laugh and a joke with them, but even though we didn't give anything away, when we got back to the hotel we didn't tell the manager!

With it being so important, the game was live on *Sky*, and knowing people were watching we wanted to play well, it added spice to the game. But the most important thing was getting that single point to guarantee our survival and confirm an even bigger achievement than the previous season when we won promotion. Adam Virgo, playing despite needing surgery on an injured knee, made a mistake early in the game which allowed Shefki Kuqi to score, but almost instantly he went down the other end and equalised from a corner to make amends.

Looking back I think it's fair to say we had our fair share of luck, but I think we played well enough to warrant the draw. The point meant that Gillingham went down, but I didn't care about that. What we hadn't realised on the pitch was how close we were to going down, with all the sides beneath doing what was required of them to overtake us if we slipped up and lost, it was frightening coming off thinking that had we made one mistake, and conceded one goal, a whole season of hard work would have been undone. I think if we had gone down a lot of people would have been released by the club, so the result prolonged a few careers.

At the final whistle the emotions were flowing. I remember our coach Bob Booker crying and everyone reacting differently. Some were ecstatic, others relieved, others exhausted. Like a boxer at the end of the first round, even as we were celebrating on the pitch at the end of the game, we knew we had it all to do again – but for the summer months it was nice to revel in the achievement ahead of the following season.

The next season we were not as fortunate. Player of the Season Adam Virgo was sold to Celtic for £1.5m, as the club really needed the cash and Adam wanted to take the opportunity on offer, while Dan Harding left for Leeds. There were a few new faces, but just as in the previous season, finances dictated that Mark was forced to gamble in search that bargain, and again all the players who arrived were unproven at Championship level. Nonetheless we had a very good first half of the season – in which we won at Crystal Palace, and that saw us with a nice cushion between ourselves and the bottom three going into the New Year. However a dreadful second half to the campaign saw us relegated a couple of games before the season finished. Losing Charlie Oatway to a broken ankle on Boxing Day was critical. He had been in superb form in the first half of the season and had he not been injured I think we would have had a much better chance of survival. Mark McGhee had done a fantastic job in getting us to the Championship and keeping us there, but he was fighting a losing battle against the better-financed clubs in the division. With the stadium issue constantly in the background and leaving the club with limited capacity at Withdean and a strain on finances it was a big ask to keep the club at that level – particularly without the likes of Charlie, Dan and Adam.

Back in League One, I played on for a couple more seasons under Mark and later Dean Wilkins and I would like to think I passed on some of my experience to the club's up-and-coming defenders at the time, such as Tommy Elphick, Joel Lynch and Adam El-Abd. In my final season 2007/08, I played most of my games alongside Tommy, before making a move into non-league football with Havant & Waterlooville, and he, along with Joel and Adam are excellent players with bright futures ahead.

I played more of my six-hundred-plus games for Brighton than any of my other clubs, and I consider them my club, but my only regret is that I didn't get a proper chance to say farewell to the Albion supporters at the end of my final season. Our last game had very little riding on it and I would have liked to have gone on for the last five minutes, but I wasn't included in the squad and it wasn't to be – but I am now back at the club and involved with the club's community scheme and am out there coaching youngsters and working to get my FA badges, as I would like to move into more senior coaching at some stage. I'm delighted to still be involved and am sure that once the new stadium has become a reality the future will be bright for Brighton.

RUSSELL SLADE
MANAGER 2009–

BORN   10 October 1960
FIRST GAME   6 March 2009
ALBION CAREER   14 games (correct to end of 2008/09 season)

In March 2009 Russell Slade inherited an Albion side who according to many were already condemned to relegation, but in a mad eight-week spell he galvanised a squad and pulled off one of the greatest escapes in the club's history. At one point, the club were eight points adrift with seven games to play, but Slade never threw in the towel and was rewarded with a five-game unbeaten run which culminated in a final-day win over Stockport County which secured Albion's League One status...

Brighton & Hove Albion 1 v Stockport County 0

League Division One
Saturday 2 May 2009

Withdean Stadium
Attendance 8,618

Brighton avoid relegation with a heroic victory

Teams

Russell Slade	Managers	Jim Gannon
Michel Kuipers		Conrad Logan
Andrew Whing		Andy Halls
Gary Borrowdale		Josh Thompson
Adam Virgo		Michael Rose
		(Sub. Greg Tansey)
Tommy Elphick		Michael Raynes
Doug Loft		Tommy Rowe
Gary Dicker		James Vincent
Dean Cox		Paul Turnbull
Tommy Fraser		Matty Mainwaring
Gary Hart		Chris O'Grady
(Sub. Calvin Andrew)		(Sub. Peter Thompson)
(Sub. Nicky Forster)		
Lloyd Owusu		Oli Johnson

Forster 73	Goal	

Referee: K Wright (Cambridgeshire)

I BEGAN MY MANAGERIAL CAREER at Notts County, after completing a degree in sports science and working in a variety of roles on the Meadow Lane coaching staff. It was also during this time that I was lucky enough to benefit from a few pearls of wisdom from the great Brian Clough, as the coaching staff at Notts County and Forest would often lunch together, and we'd always opt to go to Forest's canteen, as they served a decent cooked lunch.

In 1994/95 I was given the manager's job after Mick Walker left, becoming the youngest manager in the Football League in what is now the Championship. I took charge of the side for a few months before Howard Kendall arrived on a permanent basis and led my team out for first time at Wembley for the Anglo Italian Cup. I also worked with Howard at Sheffield United, after he took me to Bramall Lane as part of his backroom staff. Howard had wanted to take me to Everton with him, when he got the job at Goodison Park – but Sheffield United would not let me go. I also got offered the job of manager at Hull City, but Blades chairman Kevin McCabe convinced me to stay. But eventually I wanted to be a manager in my own right again, and I got my first major managerial post at Scarborough, with the Seadogs nine points adrift and facing relegation out of the Conference in October 2001.

A remarkable run of 39 points from the final 19 games lifted us to a fairly comfortable 12th place in the table and, despite the club spending much of the campaign in administration, we bettered that with a seventh-place finish the following season. After another season – in which Scarborough reached the fourth round of the FA Cup, and only lost narrowly to Chelsea – I was off to Grimsby. In my two seasons there, Grimsby enjoyed cup success, beating Spurs in the League Cup, and reached the Division Three play-off final – losing at Cardiff, 1-0 to Cheltenham.

I then moved on to Yeovil Town in the summer of 2006. Many believed Yeovil had reached the pinnacle of their ambitions, but we topped anything they had previously achieved and finished fifth in League One, and defeated promotion favourites Nottingham Forest in the play-off semi-final to reach Wembley. Winning the League One manager of the year award was no comfort after a 2-0 defeat to Blackpool at Wembley. I was at Huish Park for nearly three years, but by February 2009 it became clear I had taken Yeovil as far as I could; my ambitions for the club did not match those of the chairman and the board. There had also been some other things going on at the club and I decided it was time to leave. I had nothing lined up, but within a few days I took a call from Dick Knight.

Brighton had been expected to name Jim Gannon as their new manager, but after Gannon opted to stay at Stockport County, I suddenly found myself in the frame for the manager's job along with a few others including former MK Dons and Blackburn Rovers boss Paul Ince. After a couple of interviews with Dick I really liked what I was hearing from him, but it was obvious I would have a real job on my hands, with the team struggling in League One. I must have made a good impression too, as on the Wednesday before Brighton were due to play at Leyton Orient Dick called and I was offered the job.

Despite the club's perilous position in the League One drop zone, I felt it was a great opportunity. I signed on a short-term deal, with the incentive to keep the club in the division. I inherited a huge squad, but it was decimated by injuries and many of the players were loan signings or youngsters, but in spite of that, I still felt there was enough within the squad to keep Brighton up. I had only watched one training session ahead of my first game at Orient, so it made sense that Dean White took the team and picked the side. I was greeted by 2,000 Albion fans, desperate to see their side finally rediscover winning ways. We made a great start, with Matt Heath putting us ahead – but a penalty just before half-time and late winner from Sean Thornton left everyone deflated at full-time. With long faces in the dressing my first real job was to pick the team up for a midweek match a few days later at Withdean against in-form Southend.

We hadn't played too badly against Orient, and we weren't too bad against Southend either. They went ahead early on, but we levelled through Lloyd Owusu, who had played for me at Yeovil and had arrived at Brighton just prior to my appointment.

Again we went down to late goals, two sloppy goals to concede. In both games, against Orient and Southend, we had played okay, but we'd conceded possession cheaply, in critical areas of the pitch, and that had led to goals against. It was becoming obvious to me that this was one of the major reasons why the team were struggling at the wrong end of the table.

We immediately began working on retaining possession with the players in training and after an excellent few days on the training pitch we emphatically beat Yeovil 5-0 at Withdean. That lifted us to within three points of safety, with a game in hand. That game was on the following Tuesday evening at Walsall. While we had been putting Yeovil to the sword, they had been hammered by the same scoreline at home by Bristol Rovers.

A lot of our supporters felt we had a real opportunity to edge ourselves towards safety. I feared a backlash of some sort, and warned the players – but the performance on the night was poor; possibly the only unacceptable one during the run in to the end of the 2008/09 season. Walsall hit us with the backlash I had feared and we found ourselves deservedly 3-0 down at the interval.

For the first time I tore into the players. I was furious with them. I could take the defeats against Orient and Southend, because they'd given their all and were down to honest mistakes – but this was different. They'd ignored the advice we'd given them before the game and paid the price. They did at least stop any more goals going in after the break, but we had come into the game on a high and I had wanted the players to take the game by the scruff of the neck from the off. That didn't happen and in truth Walsall beat us up on the night. I wanted to make wholesale changes before our next game at Scunthorpe – but before that I would have to deal with a cheap shot from my former employers.

YEOVIL WERE IN THE RELEGATION SCRAP with us at the foot of the table, and after their 5-0 thumping at Withdean the previous weekend, Glovers chairman John Fry had come in for plenty of stick for letting me leave Huish Park. We'd won my last four games at Yeovil and I left them comfortably mid-table in League One. However, since I'd left they had failed to win, and the 5-0 defeat dragged them into the relegation mire.

On the Friday evening before our game at Scunthorpe, possibly in an attempt to deflect some of the flak coming his way, or maybe looking to un-settle Brighton and me, Fry issued a press statement saying the club had sacked me for gross misconduct. It was a real cheap shot. I had left by mutual consent and even agreed a settlement on the remainder of my contract!

I was absolutely furious, but refused to let it affect the team or my prepa-rations. The LMA, everyone at Brighton and Dick Knight were all extreme-ly supportive; and that evening, with the assistance of club's media depart-ment and the LMA's legal team, we drafted a statement rebutting the accu-sation. To this day I remain convinced Fry had panicked after their heavy defeat at Withdean and the subsequent criticism from the local media and Yeovil supporters.

The following day we went down 2-0 at Scunthorpe, and a few people, including a few Albion fans and the local press, were starting to write off our survival chances. A 0-0 home draw with Tranmere and 0-2 defeat at MK Dons did little to alleviate the fears and when we left Stadium MK, we were eight points adrift of safety, with seven to play. After that game I met the now-chairman Tony Bloom, and he gave me a few words of encouragement and told me we had to still believe. Most people had written us off, but like the chairman-elect I was not giving up just yet and neither were the players. All the time it was mathematically possible, we would keep plugging away.

Pos	Team	P	W	D	L	F	A	GD	Pts
17	Yeovil Town	40	11	13	16	34	57	-23	46
18	Swindon Town	41	10	15	16	60	64	-4	45
19	Carlisle United	41	11	11	19	51	65	-14	44
20	Crewe Alex	41	12	8	21	54	72	-18	44
21	Northampton Town	39	10	12	17	51	52	-1	42
22	Brighton & HA	39	8	12	19	42	62	-20	36
23	Hereford United	39	9	6	24	36	65	-29	33
24	Cheltenham Town	40	7	10	23	46	83	-37	31

On the Tuesday we travelled for a vital game at fellow-strugglers Hereford United, before an Easter Saturday visit from another team involved in the relegation shake-up Swindon Town. The target was five or six points from the next three games. Victory was achieved at Hereford, with Tommy Fraser on target with an overhead kick early on, and Lloyd Owusu putting the result beyond doubt late in the game. Lloyd was set up by Gary Hart on his return from injury, and the two instantly showed they had a real understanding and proved a vital partnership in the run in. Harty had been struggling with a knee injury for a few seasons, but now he was back to full fitness, and he was like a new signing for us, just at the right time.

Now five points adrift, we went into the Swindon game with a real incentive, and Adam Virgo put us ahead just before half-time – but a crazy 11-minute spell, early in the second half, saw Swindon go 3-1 ahead. I felt physically sick at the final whistle; I was absolutely devastated. We hadn't played badly, in truth we were the better side. And it didn't help when Swindon's management team admitted as much over the beer after the game. I just couldn't get my head around how we imploded so easily, as the old frailties were exposed. Everyone was pretty down after that game, but club physio Malcolm Stuart made the point that all we needed to do was go and win at Colchester United on Easter Monday and we'd still have the six points we'd been targeting; and to be fair to the players that was exactly what they did.

Gary Hart had been one of the bright spots in the Swindon game. Coming off the bench at 3-1 down, he had caused them more problems than anyone, and even given us brief hope late on when he created a goal for Gary Dicker which made the score 3-2. I decided to start him, and told him to give it everything for as long as he could, and then once he was out of steam to let us know and we'd get him off. Harty repaid that faith in spades as he linked up with big Lloyd once again and the two of them were superb in a 1-0 win, with the goal coming from a free-kick, won by Harty and headed in by Lloyd. As the lads came off the pitch, the results filtered in from elsewhere and made superb reading as most of our rivals had lost or drawn. Now we were three points from safety, with a game in hand. From the despondency after the defeat at Swindon, things were now looking far brighter.

A 3-1 home win over Oldham Athletic in our next game, with Harty creating Dean Cox's opening goal, and Lloyd on target twice, meant victory at Bristol Rovers the following Tuesday would finally lift us out of the drop zone. We'd hit form just at the right time, but the important thing was that we maintained that form for the final three games of the season.

Pos	Team	P	W	D	L	F	A	GD	Pts
17	Swindon Town	44	11	16	17	64	67	-3	49
18	Yeovil Town	43	12	13	18	38	61	-23	49
19	Carlisle United	44	11	13	20	53	68	-15	46
20	Crewe Alex	44	12	10	22	56	75	-19	46
- - -	- - - - - - - - -	- -	- -	- -	- -	- -	- -	- - -	- - -
21	Northampton Town	42	11	12	19	56	57	-1	45
22	Brighton & HA	43	11	12	20	50	67	-17	35
23	Cheltenham Town	43	9	11	23	50	85	-35	38
24	Hereford United	43	9	6	28	39	74	-35	33

BRISTOL WAS A SPECIAL NIGHT and one I am sure that will live in the memories of all of us who were there – but it wasn't all plain sailing. Rovers were out of the play-off chase and had little to play for; however they dominated the opening period of the game and when Rickie Lambert opened the scoring after 28 minutes, it looked like we were about to blow our golden opportunity. But within 15 minutes the Hart-Owusu combination paid dividends once again, with Harty sending in a lovely cross from the left for Lloyd to pounce at the near post.

Seven minutes into the second half Harty did it again, crossing from the right wing, and this time Calvin Andrew, on as sub for Dean Cox and playing on the left, burst into the box and headed home. 2-1 up and defending for our lives, the last ten minutes seemed to be never ending, but eventually the final whistle sparked wild celebrations in the away end and for the first time it seemed everyone believed we were going to stay up. But for myself, the staff and the players we knew we still had 180 minutes of hard work to ensure our efforts were not wasted.

We travelled to Huddersfield knowing a win might seal survival, but with the Terriers keen to send the retiring Andy Booth out on a high, we found ourselves in a really tough match at the Galpharm Stadium. With the amount of games we had played back-to-back, the players were physically drained – but they showed tremendous character as twice we fought back to draw 2-2 with Calvin and Lloyd again the scorers. That meant we were out of the relegation zone and victory against Stockport on the final day would guarantee us our League One status for 2009/10.

Lloyd grabbed deserved plaudits with his goals. He was a vital player for us, as we played a fairly direct style, with plenty of balls played up to him, but Calvin also played a vital part in survival, not least with those two goals. We had a few loan players at the club, but four were integral to the run in: Lloyd, Calvin, Gary Dicker and Gary Borrowdale. Ironically Calvin and Gary had Crystal Palace connections, but neither let that get in the way of doing a thoroughly professional job, and the Albion will always be indebted to them for their contribution. While Lloyd, at 32 years of age, was having to be wrapped up in cotton wool between games. He is a very good pro and with all his experience we let him make decisions at times: some days he didn't train and would just come in for a massage. He liked everything to be just right; you could say he was a high maintenance player, but no manager minds that if the player goes out and produces like Lloyd did week in week out, and he did just that for Brighton.

Gary Hart, such a key man in those final few games which had put us into such a good position, had limped out of the match at Huddersfield with a hamstring injury. Tests showed he had torn or pulled it and he was extremely doubtful for the Stockport game – but after a course of injections, Harty was declared fit on the morning of the game. I was confident we would get the job done, but I was never complacent and I had drilled into the players that they too had to remain focused on getting the win. They were to forget what was happening elsewhere which might man a draw would be enough to stay up, let us worry about that, and focus all their efforts on the win that would guarantee safety.

We were greeted by a sell-out crowd and as I walked out across the pitch and looked up to the south stand I felt we were going to do it – but the game wasn't without a few hiccups. First we lost Gary Hart after 17 minutes, his hamstring again the problem, and then Calvin Andrew damaged his knee just before half-time, clashing with the post as he bravely tried to put the ball into the net. I wondered if Harty had been a gamble too far.

I sent on another striker at the veteran stage of his career Nicky Forster, who despite training all week, was nowhere near match fitness, after six weeks on the sidelines. However that didn't matter ... when Stockport keeper Conrad Logan could only parry Gary Dicker's low drive, Fozzy's experience of twenty-plus years in the game put him in the right place, at the right time for a simple tap in from close range. It was possibly the easiest of Foz's 150-plus goals, but it was also one of the most important.

The final whistle confirmed our safety and signalled a huge pitch invasion from the Albion fans. They deserved their moment; after weeks adrift at the bottom the escape was complete. We all struggled to make it off to the dressing rooms and the fans wouldn't let me go before they had carried me shoulder high across the pitch. My hat got nicked and my head scratched ... but it didn't really matter (I was offered my hat back on the Monday, at the Sussex Senior Cup Final, by the fan who'd grabbed it – but I told him to keep it). When I finally got back to the office I sat there with Bob and Dean and was absolutely exhausted – both emotionally and physically. That evening we went to Malcolm Stuart's retirement bash in Hove; I was absolutely worn out and I got through the night solely on adrenalin.

Within 48 hours I was offered the manager's job permanently, and immediately accepted. My first task was to finalise a retained list, which involved some of the hardest decisions in my managerial career. There were tough decisions to be made, like releasing Doug Loft, who'd abandoned a loan spell at Dagenham & Redbridge to come back and help in the fight for survival, and Tommy Fraser, who'd also been a key player during that vital run-in and given everything for the club – but they were the right decisions at the time. Obviously of all those players who were released I want to succeed wherever their careers take them and wish them all the best.

The Stockport game, was without doubt the match of my short Albion life to date. I hope I can top that in due course, but it was an amazing climax to what I predicted when I took the job would be a mad eight-week spell ... and given my time again I don't think I would change any of it.